DOGS

A MISCELLANY

VICKY EDWARDS

summersdale

DOGS: A MISCELLANY

Summersdale Publishers Ltd
46 West Street
Chichester
West Sussex
PO19 1RP
UK

www.summersdale.com

Printed and bound in the Czech Republic

ISBN: 978-1-84953-736-0

Substantial discounts on bulk quantities of Summersdale books are available to corporations, professional associations and other organisations. For details contact Nicky Douglas by telephone: +44 (0) 1243 756902, fax: +44 (0) 1243 786300 or email: nicky@summersdale.com.

ABOUT THE AUTHOR

Vicky Edwards is a writer, actress and dog lover. A volunteer foster parent for the charity Canine Partners, Vicky lives on England's south coast with her husband, their daughter and hopefully, soon, a dog of their own.

CONTENTS

INTRODUCTION

*A dog is the only thing on earth that loves
you more than he loves himself.*

JOSH BILLINGS, AMERICAN COMEDIAN

Intelligent, loyal, affectionate, great fun and brilliant walking
buddies, dogs are indeed a joy. Willing to please and
motivated by rewards of food and/or praise, they are
also eminently trainable, which explains why there
are so many working dogs, each using their nose,
speed, brains or courage across a diverse array of
professions. From those who sniff out disease
and bombs to those four-legged superstars
who support the blind, deaf and disabled
by acting as their eyes and ears, dogs
are far more than pets to those
who depend on them.

As long-standing inspiration for artists and writers, dogs are celebrated in literature, art, film, television and song. Their cute factor also makes them a marketeer's dream, which is why some of the world's most memorable advertising campaigns feature dogs.

And for many, dogs truly are man's or woman's best friend. Always willing to cock an ear and listen to your woes or let you cuddle up to them for comfort, they are our confidantes as well as our companions: part of our family and the provider of our daily exercise.

Whether you are a dog owner or just a dog lover, this book is a salute to pups, pedigrees and mutts the world over. I hope that it will cheer, inform and entertain in equal measure.

CHAPTER 1

FROM WOLF TO MAN'S BEST FRIEND

For the strength of the Pack is the Wolf, and the strength of the Wolf is the Pack.

RUDYARD KIPLING, NOVELIST AND POET

There has been much debate over the years about the precise origins of our modern-day pooches. Scientists agree that dogs are directly descended from *Canis lupus* or, as it is more commonly known, the grey wolf, but until recently the timing and exact whereabouts of their evolution was as woolly as an Old English Sheepdog's winter coat.

In 2013, new research unveiled in *Science* magazine gave us a clearer though not entirely conclusive insight. Based on a genetic analysis of ancient and modern dog and wolf samples, a European origin was pinpointed. Early DNA studies on samples dating back some

18,000 years suggested the modern-day dog evolved from wolves that were integrated into human societies in the Middle East or possibly in East Asia as recently as 15,000 years ago. However, the 2013 analysis revealed modern dogs to be more closely related to ancient European wolves or dogs rather than to any of the farther flung wolf groups.

Ultimately the latest data suggests that dogs were domesticated far earlier than researchers had previously thought. Undertaken by Dr Olaf Thalmann, from Finland's University of Turku, the good doctor concluded that if his analysis was correct, dogs started to evolve from wolves at a time when humankind had yet to form settlements and was still sourcing food by hunting.

Because dog populations have become very mixed over time, evolving into numerous different breeds and crossbreeds and settling all over the world, it is difficult for scientists to reach a definite conclusion. Further sampling, analysis and research is needed. Additional nuclear DNA material could come up trumps but with core DNA from very old bones and fossils being tricky to retrieve, Dr Thalmann and his like have their work cut out.

Don't bite the hand that feeds you

Researchers and scientists have also turned their focus to how dogs came to be domesticated. One credible possibility is that wolves would follow hunters, probably at a distance, feasting on the scraps and carcasses left by hunters after big kills. From here perhaps they grew braver and came closer, possibly with hunters encouraging them with titbits in order to use their furry bodies as prehistoric duvets and also to rely on their acute hearing to warn them when bigger predators such as bears were near.

> ### Did you know?
>
> *The dog family (Canidae) contains all fox, wolf, coyote, jackal and dog species. Wild canids are found on every continent, with the exception of Antarctica.*

Getting to know you

Wolves may also have been encouraged into the camps of the day when human groups realised that wolves ate rats and other pests, as well as waste. No waste meant fewer flies and fewer flies meant less sickness, making groups that 'embraced' the wolves healthier and hardier than those which chased them away. Another theory is that wolf cubs proved easy to tame and that orphaned wolf pups may have been adopted into human groups. Either way, the fearsome pack animal slowly but surely became a submissive servant to its hunter master.

> ### Did you know?
>
> *The expression 'three dog night' was first coined by Inuits to describe a particularly cold night, when only the body heat of three dogs would keep you warm.*

Domestication and development

Researchers believe that the domestication of dogs happened over a period of many hundreds of years, with them gradually being bred for specific roles. Hunting was obviously the principal role for which dogs were used, leading to breeding that accentuated particular talents such as sense of smell, speed and agility, size (small enough to follow quarry into its habitat, for instance), stamina and herding instinct. But in ancient times, up to and including the Middle Ages, very few people were wealthy enough to feed a dog as we do today. Dogs had to scavenge for their own food, often living on a diet of rats. Only working dogs – sled pullers or herding dogs – would have been given food. Hunting dogs were often given scraps from their conquests, but most other dogs were entirely self-sufficient. As a result of such a diet they were often undernourished and prone to disease and infestation.

> *Recollect that the Almighty, who gave the dog to be companion of our pleasures and our toils, hath invested him with a nature noble and incapable of deceit.*
> SIR WALTER SCOTT, NOVELIST, PLAYWRIGHT AND POET

Leader of the pack to faithful servant

It is thought probable that once adopted into a human group, dogs lost their canine pack instinct and instead integrated themselves into the family groups of hunters. Perhaps this is how humans began to interact with dogs on a one-to-one basis and thus how the close relationships we have with our pet dogs today began.

One of the earliest indications that humans and dogs enjoyed a shared affection can be traced to the burial site of a woman in Israel. Dating back to approximately 11,000 BP (before present), the woman's hand is placed on the dog buried with her. Similarly, at the earliest known cemetery in Skateholm, Sweden (dating back to 5,000 BCE), there is evidence that dogs were sometimes buried with people. It is likely that these dogs were sacrificed to accompany their masters or mistresses on their journey to the afterlife. The excavation of Egyptian tombs has also revealed that dogs were mummified and buried with their masters. Some dogs were given their own grave. Buried with hunting tools, it suggests they were highly valued as hunting dogs.

Posh paws and pets

From the latter part of the Middle Ages hunting and hawking became favourite sports of the upper echelons of society. Wealthy and keen for their dogs to do better than those belonging to their fellow sportsmen, it was around this time that dogs started to be treated more like pets. Performing dogs became a much-loved source of entertainment, with jesters and fools including them in their routines. But from hunting to herding, this increased integration with human beings has taught dogs a great deal about what is expected and desired of them. And as more civilised times came to pass our canine friends continued to evolve.

One breed that has survived, albeit only just, since earliest times is the Vizsla or Hungarian Pointer. Originally the dog of the Magyar barbarian tribes that invaded central Europe during the Dark Ages, etchings dating back to the early tenth century depict a Magyar warrior and a dog resembling a Vizsla. Later adopted by Hungarian nobility, the breed all but became extinct after World War One, only surviving thanks to the efforts of Vizsla fanciers. During World War Two many Hungarians fled the Russian occupation, taking their Vizslas with them. Vizslas reappeared in the 1950s, and the breed was recognised by the American Kennel Club in 1960.

If a dog will not come to you after having looked you in the face, you should go home and examine your conscience.
WOODROW WILSON, AMERICAN PRESIDENT 1913–1921

Did you know?

In ancient Egypt, a person bitten by a rabid dog was urged to eat the liver of a dog infected with rabies to ward off the disease. The tooth of a rabid dog would also be put in a band tied to the arm of the person bitten. The menstrual blood of a bitch was used for hair removal, and dog genitals were used to prevent hair turning white. The doctor will see you now...

Breeding notes

The Dobermann Pinscher was first bred by Louis Dobermann, a tax collector. Evidently he bred the dog specifically to frighten people into paying their dues.

Also known as 'Aussie-poo', the Aussiedoodle is a Poodle-Australian Shepherd cross.

The Chinese Crested breed comes in two varieties: the Hairless and the Powder Puff.

The Labrador Retriever is the favourite breed in the USA, Canada and the UK.

The Golden Retriever originates from Scotland. During the 1860s Sir Dudley Majoribanks mated a yellow Retriever with a Tweed Water Spaniel. The result was the first 'goldie'.

Capable of a top speed of up to 72 kilometres per hour (45 miles per hour), the Greyhound is the world's fastest dog.

The Jack Russell Terrier has a bark that is certainly as big as its bite. Given its diminutive stature, this dog has a disproportionately loud voice!

To breed a St Dane you need to cross a Great Dane with a St Bernard.

Legend says that Pekinese, one of the world's oldest dog breeds and once held sacred by emperors, was the result of a liaison between a lion and a monkey.

The Newfoundland was originally bred to help fishermen drag their nets and to rescue people from drowning. Often called upon to 'doggy paddle', this incredible hound is blessed with a water-resistant coat and webbed feet. It needs to be fed more during the first year of its life, when it gains up to 45 kilograms (100 pounds), but thereafter its metabolism slows and the dog requires less food.

In the nineteenth century, Weimaraners were bred by the nobles of Weimar to hunt big game.

Chow Chows are known for their distinctive blue–black tongues. At birth, however, they have pink tongues. The change from pink to black takes place at between eight and ten weeks of age.

Bred in Germany centuries ago to hunt badgers, the Dachshund's name means 'badger dog'.

It is not only humans that need to wear sunscreen. The Mexican Hairless breed also needs to be protected from the sun's rays.

No amount of training will remove or even temper the natural hunting instinct that leads the Jack Russell. With a natural and heavily ingrained tendency to chase and kill anything that it regards as prey, smaller domestic pets will never be able to relax if they live with a Jack.

The Keeshond (pronounced KAYZ-hawnd) has been a family companion and watchdog in Holland for hundreds of years. Many Keeshonden lived on barges and farms and were used to see off vermin and provide companionship. In the eighteenth century the Keeshond became the symbol of the Dutch Patriots Party. The name was derived from the leader of this group, Kees De Gyselaer.

Loyal to Prince Llewelyn

In the village of Beddgelert, north-west Wales, a tribute to a brave and faithful hound is engraved on the supposed grave of Gelert, the famed favourite hunting dog of Prince Llewelyn. It reads:

In the thirteenth century, Llewelyn, Prince of North Wales, had a palace at Beddgelert. One day he went hunting without Gelert, who was unaccountably absent. On Llewelyn's return, the truant, stained and smeared with blood, joyfully sprang to meet his master. The prince, alarmed, hastened to find his son, and saw the infant's cot empty, the bedclothes and floor covered with blood. The frantic father plunged the sword into the hound's side thinking it had killed his heir. The dog's dying yell was answered by a child's cry. Llewelyn searched and discovered his boy unharmed, but nearby lay the body of a mighty wolf which Gelert had slain. The prince, filled with remorse, is said never to have smiled again. He buried Gelert here. The spot is called Beddgelert.

Did you know?

In 1393, the Duke of Berry, a member of the French royal family, was so touched by a dog that refused to leave its master's grave that he provided funds to keep the loyal hound fed for the rest of its days.

Royal dogs

Queen of France Marie Antoinette was, by all accounts, very fond of her Spaniel, Thisbe. Loyal and faithful Caesar, a Terrier belonging to King Edward VII, walked behind His Majesty's coffin in the funeral procession, while Her Majesty the Queen, Elizabeth II, continues the long-standing royal affection for dogs today. Royal canines span a wide variety of breeds, but it is the Corgi that most people associate with our present queen. First introduced to royal life by King George VI in 1933 when he acquired Dookie, which delighted the young princesses Elizabeth and Margaret, Dookie was joined soon by another Corgi named Jane, whose puppies Crackers and Carol also became part of the royal household. One of the Queen's favourite Corgis was Susan, who was an eighteenth birthday present.

> *I dressed dear sweet little Dash for the second time*
> *after dinner in a scarlet jacket and blue trousers.*
> QUEEN VICTORIA ON HER PET CAVALIER KING CHARLES SPANIEL

> *Here lies DASH, the Favourite Spaniel of Queen Victoria*
> *By whose command this Memorial was erected.*
> *He died on the 20 December, 1840 in his 9th year.*
> *His attachment was without selfishness,*
> *His playfulness without malice,*
> *His fidelity without deceit.*
> *READER, if you would live beloved and die*
> *regretted, profit by the example of DASH.*
> EPITAPH ON DASH'S GRAVESTONE

Did you know?

The Old Mother Hubbard of the nursery rhyme is said to be Cardinal Wolsey. The chief statesman and churchman of English Tudor history, Wolsey angered King Henry VIII when he failed to obtain the king's divorce from Catherine of Aragon. Henry was keen to divorce Catherine so that he could marry Anne Boleyn. In the famous rhyme, Henry was the 'doggie'. The 'bone' was the divorce, while the cupboard was symbolic of the Catholic Church.

During the Prince's visit, King Timahoe will be referred to only as Timahoe, since it would be inappropriate for the Prince to be outranked by a dog.

IN CORRESPONDENCE BETWEEN RICHARD NIXON AND WHITE HOUSE STAFF ON HOW TO ADDRESS THE PRESIDENT'S IRISH SETTER, KING TIMAHOE, DURING A VISIT BY PRINCE CHARLES

The cruel fate of both bull and Bulldog

Bred initially to assist in controlling livestock, Bulldogs have a history that stretches back as far as the fifth century and to an English breed called Alaunt. By the fifteenth century Bulldogs were not only used to help in farming and herding, but in a horrific pastime called bull baiting. A dog was trained to grip the ring or fixed tethering in a bull's nose and to hold fast until it had pulled the bull to the ground. The bull would often become so enraged that it would kill the dog. If the dog survived, its face was often badly injured as a result of such a barbaric bout of violence. Over time the breed's flat face – the result of being taught to grip with its nose and lower lip – became an inherited part of the dog's appearance. Bull baiting was finally banned in 1835, but tragically the idea of a dog fighting with another animal is still thought to be 'sport' in the minds of some particularly vile individuals. Illegal dog fights in which dogs are pitted against other dogs, or in some cases different animals, continue to be uncovered by animal welfare charities across the world. If you ever suspect someone of having any part in this abhorrently violent and merciless activity, do not hesitate to contact the police.

Significant dates relating to breeding and pedigree

First breeding for purpose. Greyhounds and Mastiffs were the first developed breeds; Greyhounds bred for speed and Mastiffs for protection.

Dogs first bred specifically for their hunting abilities.

First known attempt at classifying dogs by Dr John Caius in *De Canibus Britannicis*.

The Clumber Spaniel, largest of the English sporting Spaniels, is bred for the first time at Clumber Park, Nottinghamshire, England.

The Kennel Club is founded in the UK.

The American Kennel Club is founded.

Charles Cruft stages the first Crufts dog show at the Royal Agricultural Hall, Islington, London with 2,437 entries and 36 breeds attending.

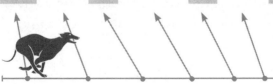

| 3,000–4,000 years ago | Middle Ages | 1570 | 1770 | 1873 | 1884 | 1891 |

*I wonder if other dogs think poodles are
members of a weird religious cult.*

RITA RUDNER, AMERICAN WRITER, COMEDIAN AND ACTRESS

Bark when your breed is called out

It is estimated that there are as many as 800 distinct recognised breeds worldwide (different countries have different criteria for the recognition of different breeds). Each breed has its own particular characteristics.

A description of the traits and features of every breed is laid down by organisations such as the UK's Kennel Club, including so-called 'designer' dogs, like the Puggle, which is a cross between a Pug and a Beagle.

The Kennel Club UK has agreements with over 40 Kennel Clubs around the world. Other similar organisations around the globe also manage breed registers. In most instances new breeds are considered for recognition once there are specimens of it in its country of origin.

List of clubs with which the Kennel Club has full reciprocal agreements outside the UK

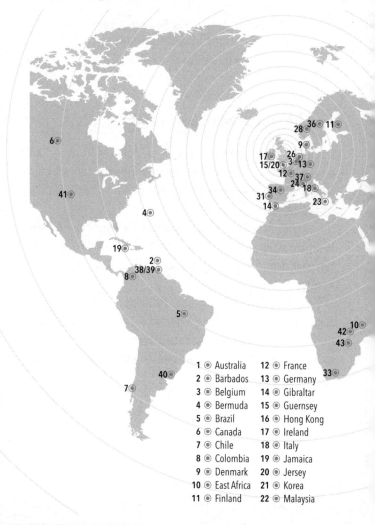

1 ⦿ Australia		**12** ⦿ France	
2 ⦿ Barbados		**13** ⦿ Germany	
3 ⦿ Belgium		**14** ⦿ Gibraltar	
4 ⦿ Bermuda		**15** ⦿ Guernsey	
5 ⦿ Brazil		**16** ⦿ Hong Kong	
6 ⦿ Canada		**17** ⦿ Ireland	
7 ⦿ Chile		**18** ⦿ Italy	
8 ⦿ Colombia		**19** ⦿ Jamaica	
9 ⦿ Denmark		**20** ⦿ Jersey	
10 ⦿ East Africa		**21** ⦿ Korea	
11 ⦿ Finland		**22** ⦿ Malaysia	

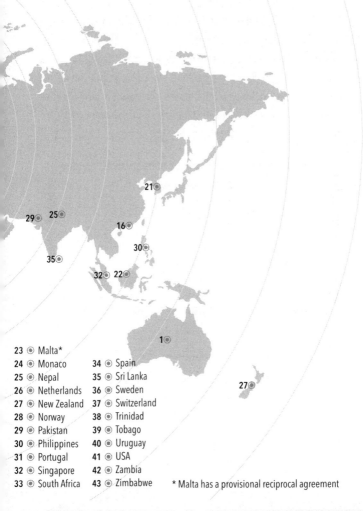

23 ⊙ Malta*
24 ⊙ Monaco
25 ⊙ Nepal
26 ⊙ Netherlands
27 ⊙ New Zealand
28 ⊙ Norway
29 ⊙ Pakistan
30 ⊙ Philippines
31 ⊙ Portugal
32 ⊙ Singapore
33 ⊙ South Africa

34 ⊙ Spain
35 ⊙ Sri Lanka
36 ⊙ Sweden
37 ⊙ Switzerland
38 ⊙ Trinidad
39 ⊙ Tobago
40 ⊙ Uruguay
41 ⊙ USA
42 ⊙ Zambia
43 ⊙ Zimbabwe

* Malta has a provisional reciprocal agreement

The language of dogs

The expression 'black dog', used to describe depression, conjures up a powerful image: a dark and shadowy figure that lurks; an ever-present but unwelcome guest; that if it were to pounce, could destroy you. A figure long since associated with fear, in folklore and myth, black dogs in dreams are thought to represent death. Famously referred to by Sir Winston Churchill, twice prime minister of the UK, to describe his bouts of gloom, the expression is now common parlance and is often used to articulate a feeling of downheartedness, inexplicable sadness or negativity.

Collective canines

- *Kennel: dogs in general*
- *Cowardice: curs and mongrels*
- *Pack, cry or mute: hounds*
- *Litter: puppies*
- *Pack: wild dogs*

Buy a pup and your money will buy love
unflinching that cannot lie.
RUDYARD KIPLING, 'THE POWER OF THE DOG'

CHAPTER 2

HOW MUCH IS THAT DOGGIE IN THE WINDOW? BECOMING A DOG OWNER

*The only creatures that are evolved enough to
convey pure love are dogs and infants.*

JOHNNY DEPP, ACTOR AND MUSICIAN

Having your own dog brings many rewards, but should not be entered into without due consideration. Be as certain as is possible that having a dog full-time will work for you, researching all the aspects of dog ownership before you make a canine commitment.

Excluding Russia, there are around 70 million pet-owning households across Europe. According to the European Pet Food Federation just over half of this estimation includes an almost equal split of cats (25 per cent) and dogs (26 per cent). Over half of all American households now have at least one cat or dog at home. In 2012 the Pet Food Institute (PSI) in America estimated that the pet dog population had reached more than 75 million in the USA.

The top five reasons given for owning a dog

1 Companionship

2 Long-held wish (by adult or child)

3 Believed that it is easy to care for and look after

4 Rescued from poor or unsafe circumstances

5 Fits in with the lifestyle of owner/s

Pedigree or pooch?

The advantage of buying a pedigree dog means you have access to its history. You can also easily find out the particulars and peculiarities of the breed that takes your fancy, making it easier to make an informed choice when it comes to matching a dog to your lifestyle. With a pedigree dog everything from its temperament, likely ailments and more can be explored in advance of becoming a dog owner. With a mutt or pooch this is obviously more difficult, especially if you do not know what breeds it is a cross between. That said, don't be put off by mutts, especially those looking for homes via a rescue centre. In most instances staff at such centres will fully assess dogs before re-homing them, taking careful note of their behavioural tendencies, exercise requirements and character traits, as well as having them examined by a vet. These dogs are usually so happy to find a 'forever' home that what they lack in pedigree they make up with in unconditional love. Whichever you choose, finding out as much as you can about a dog before committing to add it to your family is essential.

Did you know?

Small dogs generally don't need as much exercise as larger breeds, but remember that you may have to carry them if they get tired. Carrying even a weeny 'handbag' dog for any distance is hard work.

Which bitch?

> *Dogs are not our whole life,*
> *but they make our lives whole.*
>
> ROGER A. CARAS, AMERICAN WILDLIFE PHOTOGRAPHER AND WRITER

Choosing the breed that best fits in with you and your family is not just important for humans; it's important for the dog, too. There's no point buying a Bulldog if you're looking for a dog to accompany you on marathon training. If you know that you need a dog that will flourish in a noisy family home then breeds such as the Irish Setter, Golden Retriever or Labrador are among those best suited to you. If walking is your thing then a Collie will happily match you step for step, while for companionship without too much schlepping Bulldogs and Borzois should be a good match. Pugs and Sussex Spaniels are among the breeds best suited to first-time dog owners. Dogs that don't moult are often best for those with allergies, although you should speak to your doctor before getting a dog if you are routinely bothered by conditions such as asthma.

Ultimately, if you are contemplating dog ownership then you must first make an honest list of the ways in which having a dog will impact on your life. How much time you will be able to spend at home is a key point, as is how much time, daily, you can commit to 'walkies'. If you travel a lot then ask yourself if perhaps you would be better signing up to one of the many dog fostering schemes instead. These schemes enable you to enjoy the benefits of having a dog around, but at times when you can give it the love and attention it deserves.

Golden rules when choosing a dog

Make your choice a completely realistic one that is based on your lifestyle and your family.

Research thoroughly and obtain your dog through a well-regulated source, be that a reputable breeder or a dog re-homing charity.

Be cautious of small ads and social media advertising dogs for sale. You need proof of the dog having had its inoculations and you need to be certain that the dog is legally theirs to part with – sadly, the number of dogs reported as missing is on the increase.

Never choose a dog based purely on its appearance. No matter how much it looks at you with big, sad eyes.

Did you know?

The Kennel Club holds an annual Puppy Awareness Week (PAW) to help promote puppy welfare. PAW aims to make sure that pups live healthy, happy lives with suitable owners and to stamp out puppy farming. To be absolutely sure of the breeder's credentials, and to be confident that the welfare of the dogs and puppies has been prioritised, always check with the Kennel Club for confirmation of their registered breeders. Puppy farming is horrific, and while there are people willing to turn a blind eye in order to get themselves a cheaper puppy (that is likely to be prone to illness and disease as a result of being kept in poor and in some cases utterly grim conditions), the practice will continue. Be part of the solution rather than the problem.

At my feet and in my heart
By my side o'er field and sand
Never was a man so loyal
Give me the dog, not golden band.

ANONYMOUS

Preparing your home for a dog

Before you bring a dog into your home you need to get organised and prepare for its arrival. Pet stores may leave you baffled – there is a vast array of products and toys on the market – but there are some basics that you will need.

If you are getting a puppy or a rescue dog that has not been trained then you also need to think about protecting your home. When a puppy's teeth come through it may chew furniture, so consider baby gates to keep it out of rooms where it could do real damage to precious furniture or belongings. A puppy will also widdle all over the place until it is house-trained so plan ahead and store up a good supply of newspaper.

> *If there are no dogs in Heaven, then when I*
> *die I want to go where they went.*
> WILL ROGERS, ACTOR, HUMORIST AND SOCIAL COMMENTATOR

Did you know?

Canine parvovirus is a virus that can survive in the environment for months or even years. First coming to light as an epidemic in the 1970s, thousands of dogs died before a vaccine became available. The parvovirus is still fairly common in unvaccinated dogs, so protecting your dog through vaccination is crucial.

Canine kit shopping list

A comfy and appropriately-sized basket (with room for the dog to grow)
Bedding (machine washable and non-allergenic)
Grooming equipment and dog shampoo

Food recommended by your vet
Water and feed bowls
Poo bags

Leads (one short and one retractable)
Collar
Travel harness and travel crate

Microchip
Identity disc (only list your telephone number, not the dog's name)
Pet insurance

Appropriate toys approved for dogs

Get grooming

Depending on their coat, some dogs will need the ministrations of a professional groomer. Long-haired dogs especially will need more frequent grooming, but even short-haired dogs need a sprucing routine. Some benefits of grooming your dog are:

- it aerates his coat, promoting healthy growth.
- it is good for his circulation.
- it helps to keep grease levels down and therefore prevents the formation of sebaceous cysts as a result of blocked pores.
- it prevents matted fur, which can drag on the skin causing soreness.
- it gives you the chance to check him for any wounds, cuts or problems such as fleas or ticks.
- it reduces his stress levels and aids the bond between you.

Hairy feet can mean that long claws are missed. You should check your dog's claws weekly. Unless a dog has a particular skin complaint and you have been advised by a vet to do so, there is no need to bathe your dog. If he has rolled in fox poo, however, the 'need' is yours – you will certainly want to give the mucky pup a doggy shampoo to wash away the horrible pong.

Dog ownership and the law

Under British law it is illegal for your dog to be dangerously out of control in any public place, in a neighbour's home or even in your own home. You could also be in trouble with the police if your dog injures someone, makes someone fear that they will be injured or attacked by your dog, or if your dog causes an accident. In some instances you could even face a custodial sentence. It is also worth noting that farmers are permitted to shoot dogs if they are worrying livestock, so do take care and be responsible when walking in the countryside.

In the UK from 2016 you will be required by law to have your dog microchipped. Having a microchip means that a dog can be swiftly reunited with its owner in the event that the dog goes missing. Have your dog chipped by a local vet and don't be tempted by some of the 'home chipping' kits that you may see advertised on the internet.

Lost and found

If you find a dog without an owner then it is your duty (if not legally in some countries then certainly morally) to return the dog to its owner or report it to the local authority. If you don't do this and try to keep the dog, this could constitute theft. If no owner is found, you may be allowed to keep the dog, but there is the possibility that the original owner could still claim it. If you lose your dog you should immediately inform the local authority.

Gratitude: that quality which the canine mongrel seldom lacks; which the human mongrel seldom possesses!
LION P. S. REES

Banned dogs

Some countries have a 'banned dogs' list. In the UK, for example, the following dogs are banned and may not be owned:

- Pit Bull Terrier
- Japanese Tosa
- Dogo Argentino
- Fila Braziliero

It's also against the law to sell, abandon, give away or breed from a banned dog. A banned dog can be seized by the police or the dog warden even if it hasn't displayed dangerous behaviour and no complaint has been recorded.

In the USA certain breeds may be banned in different states and cities, while in Spain certain breeds are banned from private ownership unless they are licensed and controlled. Other countries have similar laws so wherever you are in the world, make sure that you learn the law of the land before you acquire a dog and ensure that you buy a dog from a reputable source.

Did you know?

Over half of all American households now have at least one cat or dog sharing their home.
Source: PFMA.org.uk

Europe: a continent of pet lovers

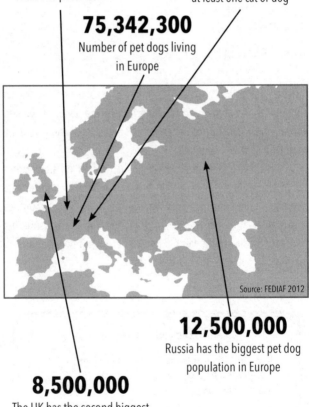

72 million
Number of European
households owning at
least one pet animal

24 per cent
Estimated percentage of
European households owning
at least one cat or dog

75,342,300
Number of pet dogs living
in Europe

Source: FEDIAF 2012

12,500,000
Russia has the biggest pet dog
population in Europe

8,500,000
The UK has the second biggest
pet dog population in Europe

Children and other animals

Puppies are easier to socialise with children and other pets, but care needs to be taken when introducing a pup into your family. Children should be encouraged to read (or have read to them) suitably targeted books about caring for a dog, and if possible to be included in puppy training classes. They should know not to treat the puppy as a toy and never to disturb it when it is eating, sleeping or going to the toilet. Toddlers may be inclined to romp with a puppy, causing both to become overexcited and most likely causing the puppy to unintentionally nip. If you have a toddler and a puppy then it is only fair to both that they are under adult supervision at all times when together. Never leave a dog and a small child alone together, regardless of the age of pup, dog, baby or tot. Teach children to be patient with and kind to all animals, and never to tease a dog or deliberately try to make it jealous. In the UK the law states that children must be ten years of age before they are allowed to be responsible for a dog outside their home, so don't give in to the pleading of younger children to be allowed to take the family dog for a walk, even if it is only around the block. Different countries have different laws about dog ownership. Make sure that you are familiar with these, wherever your home country is. All families should agree a list of doggy rules before a dog joins the family. Consistency is crucial to a dog learning what is and isn't acceptable behaviour and a unified approach is more effective and far easier for your pooch to understand.

Puppy development

Happiness is a warm puppy.
CHARLES M. SCHULZ, CREATOR OF THE *PEANUTS* CARTOONS

birth
A puppy is born blind, deaf and toothless
and totally dependent on its mother

week 1
A puppy will sleep for 90
per cent of the time

weeks 2-3
Pup begins to see and hear, and
will stand for the first time

weeks 3-4
Pup starts to play with its
brothers and sisters

week 4
Pup stops nursing and
starts to eat solid food

Birth to 12 months: a rough timeline

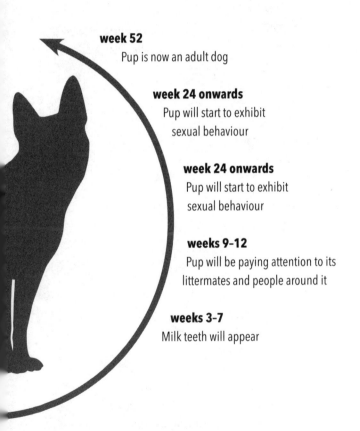

week 52
Pup is now an adult dog

week 24 onwards
Pup will start to exhibit
sexual behaviour

week 24 onwards
Pup will start to exhibit
sexual behaviour

weeks 9-12
Pup will be paying attention to its
littermates and people around it

weeks 3-7
Milk teeth will appear

Anatomy of a dog

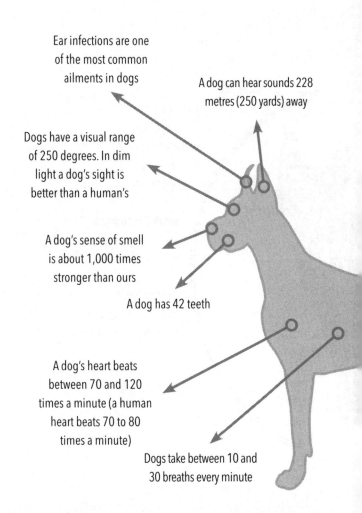

Ear infections are one of the most common ailments in dogs

A dog can hear sounds 228 metres (250 yards) away

Dogs have a visual range of 250 degrees. In dim light a dog's sight is better than a human's

A dog's sense of smell is about 1,000 times stronger than ours

A dog has 42 teeth

A dog's heart beats between 70 and 120 times a minute (a human heart beats 70 to 80 times a minute)

Dogs take between 10 and 30 breaths every minute

A dog's temperature is usually between 37.9–39.3 °C (100.2–102.8 °F)

High-fibre, low-fat diets are believed to be beneficial to dogs suffering with pancreatitis

The gestation period is 60 days

Used for communication, scent spreading and as a counterbalance

Dogs sweat through their pads and feet

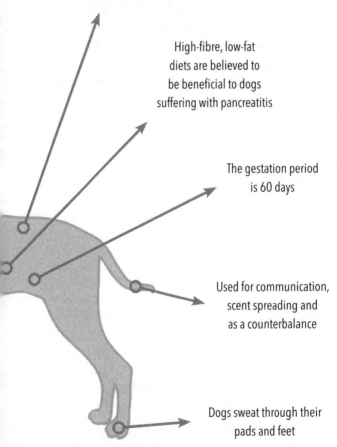

Staying safe

Since 2005 there have been 17 deaths due to dog attacks in the UK, while in the USA there were 42 fatalities as a result of dog bites recorded in 2014 alone. More than 200,000 people a year are estimated to be bitten by dogs in England (compared to 4.5–4.7 million Americans), with the annual cost to the National Health Service of treating injuries being approximately three million pounds. Hospital admissions owing to dog bites have also risen. In almost all cases vicious dogs are dogs that have either been ill-treated or whose needs are not being met, for example with insufficient exercise, diet or living conditions. Teach children to be cautious around dogs they don't know, no matter how friendly looking the dog may be. Never go to stroke, pet or feed a dog that you meet without first checking with the owner that it is safe to do so.

If you suspect any dog of being treated cruelly then call the RSPCA immediately. The RSPCA estimates that, on average, someone in England and Wales telephones their 24-hour cruelty line (0300 1234 999) every 30 seconds. In the USA, contact your local ASPCA (www. aspca.org).

Did you know?

In the USA, of the dogs entering shelters, approximately 35 per cent are adopted, 31 per cent are euthanised and 26 per cent that came in as strays are returned to their owner.

Name, don't shame

Before bringing your new pup or dog home, it will need a name (if it hasn't already been given one). Make sure it's not something that you will feel daft yelling in public, nor a handle that is likely to be so common that there will be a host of dog owners all hollering the same name in the park.

Top ten names for dogs in 2014

🇬🇧	🇺🇸
Poppy	Bella
Alfie	Max
Molly	Buddy
Bella	Lucy
Charlie	Daisy
Daisy	Molly
Millie	Bailey
Ruby	Maggie
Lola	Charlie
Oscar	Sadie
Source: John Lewis Pet Insurance	Source: www.theilovedogsite.com

Introducing a puppy or dog to other pets

Bringing a new puppy into a home that already has pets in residence demands a mix of sensitivity and common sense. Here are some basic dos and don'ts.

☑ DO give first preference to existing pet residents. Your pup will know no different and will not be regarded as a threat by your other animals. Feed other pets first and greet and play with them ahead of the newbie. If your other pet is an older dog, be sure to let it pass through doors and on the stairs ahead of the other.

☒ DON'T allow a puppy to hijack your attention when you are interacting with other pets.

☑ DO bring your puppy into the room of any existing pet after feeding and playtime. If the puppy or dog is calm it is more likely to simply settle in the room and sleep or chew on a toy. Stay in the room and sit close to the cage, stroking your dog in a relaxed way. Do this daily in the initial introductory period.

☒ DON'T think that shoving a new puppy or dog in with existing pets will result in them just getting along. Keep your new puppy in a cordoned-off area (preferably not a space that has previously been used as a feeding area for your other pets). If you have to move existing caged pets in order to do this, make sure you do it at least a week prior to the new arrival, as this way they won't associate the newcomer with any sort of upheaval.

☑ DO introduce an existing dog to a newcomer on neutral territory, if at all possible (a car park or quiet field are good spots). If this isn't possible, bring your existing hound out into the garden to be introduced. If your newcomer is a puppy, have someone else with the puppy, on a lead, as you calmly approach with your dog at a relaxed pace and on a loose lead. Have treats for your dog and keep your attention firmly on him. If your dog seems calm and happy then ask your puppy handler to carry the new dog into your house.

☒ DON'T force the issue. If your dog's reaction falls way short of rolling out the red carpet, start off with the puppy in a playpen and interact with your dog as if the pup was not there. Stay calm and gradually allow them to get used to each other.

☑ DO, if you already have a cat at home, expect it to give a new puppy a wallop on the nose! Start off the introductions by popping the pup in a cage or crate with a few of its favourite toys and then let your cat wander around it. Step in only if the puppy gets hysterical and needs calming. When you feel that your cat is used to the presence of the puppy, move on to putting pup on a lead and bringing it into the same room as the cat. At this point it is likely that the wallop from puss will be forthcoming, just to put the dog in its place and to warn it not to get too boisterous.

Part-time dogs

If you find dog ownership doesn't fit with your lifestyle – and as a genuine dog lover, you would never have a dog without being able to give it all the time and attention that it needs – then you could consider fostering or puppy parenting. Many dog rescue organisations, sanctuaries and centres that train working dogs such as disability assistance dogs are often looking for short-term fosterers, giving you all the pleasure of having a four-legged friend around, but at times to suit.

You will need a secure garden (although not necessarily a big one) and to agree to abide by any conditions laid down by the organisation lending you a canine house guest. You may also be required to attend a training course where you will learn the commands the dog is used to, as well as their routines.

Puppy parenting for organisations that train dogs for a specific purpose is more of a commitment. It generally entails looking after a puppy from the time it is separated from its mother to the point it begins its advanced training. You may have to agree to take pup to weekly basic training classes, as well as undertaking jobs such as house-training. And then of course you do have to say goodbye to it after a few months, by which time you may well have become very attached to your little bundle of furry joy. In most cases, though, organisations and charities will gladly give you a new puppy with which to wipe away your tears.

CHAPTER 3

BEST BEHAVIOUR

*Just being with dogs, I learned their ways and began
to appreciate things from their point of view.*

CESAR MILLAN, DOG WHISPERER AND DOG TRAINER

There's more to dog ownership than simply loving and looking after your pooch. Like parenthood, tough love is sometimes needed to ensure that safety lessons are thoroughly learnt, while socialising and house-training are also important – for you and your dog. You need to be prepared to work at training your dog, and to be patient.

Training your dog

Ideally a dog should attend training classes from puppyhood. Attending such classes helps to socialise your puppy and helps you to have a clear understanding of the moral responsibilities of dog ownership. A puppy should also be introduced to a broad spectrum of adults and children and other animals. Take care not to do too much too soon or you will simply frighten or confuse the pup, but try to do a little each week to familiarise it with new experiences and new people. Do remember, however, that a puppy may be unprotected from some canine diseases until it is fully vaccinated. Check with your vet before embarking on training of any kind. For details of classes in your area speak to your vet, or visit the websites of organisations such as the RSPCA, ASPCA or Kennel Club.

Training a dog from a puppy gives you the best chance of having a sociable and relaxed dog. After three months it is more difficult to train a dog, since after this point it will have already learnt to be fearful in certain situations. But if you acquire an older dog, don't worry; training is still worth the effort, but it may take you longer than with a pup. There are training classes for dogs of all ages – don't believe the old adage about old dogs and new tricks! – and the great advantages of such classes is that you will not only have a well-trained dog, but you'll meet other dog lovers and thus build up your own local network of fellow dog walkers and potential dog-sitters.

Speak to your vet for guidance on the best ways to socialise your dog, although do bear in mind that a puppy can't be taken out until it has had all its vaccinations. However, it may be viable to expose it to experiences outside of the home – say, traffic noise – by taking it out in a pet carrier, thus enabling the pup to absorb smells and sounds and to make contact with people in a controlled way. But do take professional advice so that your dog is not in any way vulnerable to infection.

Once the puppy has had all its injections, the job of socialisation should continue. The more experiences you can expose it to in its early life, the more you will build your pet's confidence. With all new experiences, ensure that you make your dog feel secure by being firmly in control. If the puppy senses your anxiety then it will pick up on your fear. Keep such sessions short, and always reward your dog when it behaves well.

Why does watching a dog be a dog fill one with happiness?
JONATHAN SAFRAN FOER, AUTHOR OF *EVERYTHING IS ILLUMINATED*

Puppy meet and greet

The following are places, people and situations that you should introduce to your puppy, on a short lead where appropriate:

- Other animals
- Children
- People of different ethnicities
- People wearing uniforms and headwear (helmets, turbans and caps, for example)
- Travelling by car in its harness or crate
- Travelling on public transport
- Busy parks
- The beach
- The high street
- Traffic noise and vehicles such as dust carts, motorcycles, emergency vehicles and buses
- The noise of domestic appliances

'Better go now!'

Toilet training your puppy is generally a fairly straightforward process, but a routine, created around your pup's body clock, is essential. A puppy usually wees as soon as it wakes up, so be ready to take him into the garden as soon as he stirs. Weeing within a quarter of an hour of eating is also usual, and pooing within half an hour. It does of course vary from dog to dog, but these are general guidelines.

These little bundles of canine joy do have pretty poor bladder control while they are infants and they may well need to wee hourly. Take pup to its toileting area frequently and praise and reward him when he does his business outside. The toileting area should be a part of your garden that you are happy to dedicate to your dog as its loo, ideally a grassed area. By continually taking it to the same spot a pup will soon recognise that this is where it 'goes'. Overexcited pups will make puddles wherever they are, so keep a cloth and disinfectant handy. It may be a good idea to keep a record of your puppy's toileting routine until you are familiar with a pattern. Use cues like 'better go now' or 'busy time' when they are toileting, so they start to associate the action with your words. By introducing your puppy to toileting in the garden early on you will hopefully minimise accidents in the house. Overnight it makes sense to put plenty of newspaper down in the puppy's sleeping area or crate, as little bladders won't be able to last all night without relief.

Crate training

Dogs like to have a den-like space, and a crate not only provides such a space, but can also assist with toilet training. Somewhere your pet can escape to when it needs a bit of peace, a crate should be small and cosy, but big enough for your dog to turn around in comfortably.

Dogs naturally prefer a clean bed, so a crate is a space that they will only soil if they are desperate. Don't put newspaper down in the crate, as this will encourage pup to toilet there. Instead, place paper outside the crate – in the kitchen or laundry room or wherever your pup spends most time.

When your puppy or untrained dog is unsupervised it should be in the crate (although not for extended periods, apart from overnight). The dog should learn to go into the crate by following a cue word such as 'bed'. Reward your dog with a treat and it will soon associate the space with somewhere safe that also earns it a reward for spending time there. Initially just reward your dog for going in, wait a few moments and then release it again. Praise and pet your dog for doing what is asked of it. Build up the time it spends in the crate gradually.

Be sure never to send it to the crate as a form of punishment as this gives your dog a very mixed message and will confuse it. If it cries to be let out, gently tap on the crate and say 'quiet'. Don't give in and let your dog out, as this will lead it to conclude that crying is a behaviour that will be rewarded. If it goes to the toilet indoors or in the crate, take your dog directly outside to its toilet area and give your regular command for toileting.

There are also various toileting aids on the market that some dog owners find helpful, but there are just as many common mistakes made by well-meaning dog owners when it comes to toilet training and you are well advised to take advice from your vet, breeder or qualified websites where plenty of information is available from organisations like the Kennel Club.

Woofs and words

Some canine experts believe that the average dog can understand approximately 160 words. Like little children learning to talk, repetition and consistency are key. If you call your dog's food 'din dins' and others in your household call it something different then it may be slow to catch on (until you reach for the food itself). Everyone needs to use the same words and tone when referring to events and objects or giving commands that you want your furry friend to become familiar with.

Start with its name and everyday commands and see how many words you can add to its vocabulary – although you'll have to go some way to beat the likes of Rico and Chaser. Rico, a Border Collie, appeared on a German television game show in 2001 and proved that he could recognise 200 words. Rico held the record until Chaser, another Border Collie, raised the bar by demonstrating knowledge of an incredible 1,022 words! Chaser's owner began training Chaser in 2004, teaching her the names of up to two items every day.

Did you know?

Fifi Geldof, eldest daughter of Sir Bob Geldof, is a dog lover who believes that every dog should have his or her day – birthday, that is. When her Spaniel-Collie cross puppy Lola reached her first birthday, Fifi and husband Andrew threw a pup play-date party on London's Clapham Common for all of Lola's friends.

Lost in translation

Humans misinterpret much of a dog's body language. Yawning, for instance, is more likely to be suggesting that it is stressed or confused than weary. Licking its lips when it isn't close to feeding time is a signal that suggests the dog is uncomfortable in some way, while shaking as if it had just emerged dripping wet from a pond is a dog's way of communicating that it needs to settle down. Repeatedly scratching its collar area is more likely to indicate stress, rather than an itch.

Said to be as intelligent as the average toddler, dogs are sensitive and empathetic. When you are sad your dog will immediately read this and adapt its behaviour, mirroring your emotion; becoming mournful, losing its appetite and being disinterested in toys. Your dog may well come and lie at your feet or rest a paw or its head on your lap. In a report published in the journal *Animal Cognition*, researchers claimed that a dog was more likely to approach someone in tears than someone who was humming. The research also established that a dog's response to crying was generally submissive behaviour.

A whiff of danger

With its turbo-charged sense of smell a dog can sniff out adrenalin, a smell it links with fear and danger. If you are scared, your dog will be on red alert. Big breeds like Rottweilers or Dobermanns will be ready to leap to your aid and bring down anyone posing a threat. Smaller dogs, or those with nervous dispositions, will start to mirror your fear and will become visibly anxious, panting and pacing or possibly seeking to hide themselves. Lead by example! If you want your dog to be brave, you will have to exhibit fearlessness.

Like and lick, or sneer and snarl?

When we look at someone we love our body has a chemical reaction, releasing dopamine and serotonin into our system, which prompts feelings of happiness. The same thing happens when you look upon someone you dislike, except that the body releases a different set of hormones that are associated with negative emotions – hatred, fear and resentment. Your dog reads these hormonal changes, and if you dislike someone your dog will almost certainly show similar disdain for the person concerned.

> ### Did you know?
>
> *There is no hard evidence that dogs can sense when a woman is pregnant, but there are plenty of accounts from women who saw changes in their dog's behaviour during their pregnancy. Many claim that their dog suddenly became much more protective and affectionate. Given their amazing sense of smell it is entirely plausible that the dogs can detect the hormonal changes caused by pregnancy.*

Don't hug a pug!

Just like us – or most of us, at least – dogs need and thrive on affection and positive interaction. A kind voice, a tummy rub, a gentle romp, its back patted or a scratch under the chin – your dog will soon show you what its favourite form of physical contact is. In almost all cases, dogs dislike being hugged or cuddled. It may feel very natural to us, but a tight embrace is restrictive and alarming for them.

Dogs don't rationalise. They don't hold anything against a person. They don't see the outside of a human but the inside of a human.

CESAR MILLAN

Pushing the boundaries

Dogs like to test us. If they find someone who does not punish them for stealing the cat's dinner or destroying a cushion, they will push the boundaries  even further. Dogs depend on your being their pack leader and dictating what is OK and what is not, so it's up to you to be the alpha male, even if you're a seven-stone girlie-girl. Be firm but fair, and don't allow bad habits such as feeding your dog from the table or allowing it up on your bed. If your dog misbehaves, chastise it firmly.

Dogs behaving badly

Dogs that jump up at people usually do so because they are excited or because they want to say a friendly hello. Early training helps prevent this from becoming a habit. The best way is simply to ignore them. Don't meet their eyes, don't push them away and don't speak to them. If they continue, walk away. If you push them away they will think it's a game.

If a dog displays fear at something irrational (thunder and firework noises are two common dog fears), be sure to ignore it. Reassurance and trying to soothe the dog simply reinforces the idea that there is something to be scared of. Talk calmly and let the dog hide itself under a chair or table (which it will usually do in such circumstances) but carry on as normal with whatever you are doing. If your dog sees you unconcerned by whatever it is that's freaking it out, your dog will gradually learn that its fear is misplaced.

The vet: friend, not foe

To get your dog used to the vet and to stop the dog developing a fear – or even a phobia – about going to see the man in the mask, try to acclimatise your dog by taking it on visits when nothing is done; no jabs, no prodding and nothing lopped off. Regularly inspecting your dog's mouth and paws is good practice anyway, but it will also get it used to being handled in a way that the vet is likely to need to do.

> *If you think dogs can't count, try putting three dog biscuits in your pocket and then give Fido only two of them.*
> PHIL PASTORET, AMERICAN WRITER AND AUTHOR

Ouch! Nipping it in the bud

Puppies, like babies, explore the world with their mouths. Teach your pup early on what it is OK to chew (their toys) and what is not (you, your belongings and your clothes). You and your family must accept that if you don't tidy up after yourselves then a puppy or a dog that is prone to picking things up (Retrievers are shocking for nicking knickers, socks and shoes that are left lying around!) will consider anything that they find fair game. If you don't want to be wearing crotchless pants or toeless socks, be mindful about putting things in their proper place or out of reach.

One of the best ways to teach a pup not to bite is to firstly let it know when it has hurt you. Saying 'Ouch!' loudly, turning away from the culprit and stopping play for a few minutes will let it know that the playful nip it just gave you wasn't OK. You can also encourage better behaviour by using a dog treat. Hold the treat in your hand, your fingers wrapped around it tightly. If your dog tries to bite, paw or force it out of your hand, don't give it the treat. Wait until it takes its nose and mouth away from your hand and then give it the treat, with lots of praise. This way your dog learns that its teeth making contact with human skin is not to its advantage.

Did you know?

In 2011 Laura Hothersall from Wiltshire, England, told a national newspaper that her Boxer, Harvey, enjoyed fine dining: organic dog biscuits, organic sirloin steak and a full roast dinner on Sundays. Harvey ate like a king. Ms Hothersall, on the other hand, having spent all her money on her beloved pooch, presumably lived on bread and jam.

A dog's dinner

I gazed at the plate, empty on one side. I was sure there had been a sausage left. And where was Monty? I leaned over the arm of the chair to look round the room. There, under the table, half-hidden by a tablecloth, I could see an enormous black dog, silently licking his lips.

BARRIE HAWKINS, *TWENTY WAGGING TALES: OUR YEAR OF REHOMING ORPHANED DOGS*

When you acquire a new dog or puppy, investigate its diet and what suits its digestive system. A good breeder will always give you comprehensive information about a pup's diet and digestion; shelters and rescue centres will be able to give you as much information as they have been able to glean, depending on how long the dog has been with them.

The rule of thumb is not to give your dog much (if any) variety, instead sticking to food that is easily digested and results in dark brown, firm poo. Check with your vet or local pet-food shop if you need more advice and help. Change your dog's diet only on the advice of your vet, with dietary changes taking place gradually over a fortnight in order to minimise digestive upsets. Always dispose of food that is left in the dog's bowl 20 minutes after feeding time, as this avoids infection through flies laying eggs in the leftover food. Ensure that your dog always has access to clean water.

Train your dog to wait nicely for its food. You should be able to tell it to sit, and then you should put the dish down and count to five. When you have reached the count of five, make eye contact with your dog and give a cue such as 'OK' so that it knows it can chow down. Training classes will help enormously with table manners, such as waiting for food rather than jumping up to get to the grub before it is even in the bowl!

Some food and drink can be very dangerous for dogs to consume. The list is fairly extensive so do your homework on this aspect of canine care thoroughly.

Not on the menu!

Never give a dog (or leave anywhere accessible to a dog) any of the following:

 Alcohol – it can affect coordination and cause breathing difficulties, abnormal acidity and even death.

 Apple seeds – the case surrounding the actual seed is toxic to dogs as it contains a natural chemical that releases cyanide when digested.

 Avocado – this contains persin, which is known to cause diarrhoea, vomiting, and heart congestion.

 Cat food – the protein and fat levels in cat food are too high for dogs.

 Chewing gum and sweets containing sugar – as with humans, sugar can lead to hyper behaviour and, over time, result in diseases such as diabetes. Gum also often contains an ingredient that can lead to kidney failure.

 Chocolate – this not only contains harmful levels of caffeine and can cause vomiting and diarrhoea and damage the heart and nervous system, but also theobromine and theophylline, which can be toxic.

Cooked bones – these can splinter when chewed, causing choking and asphyxiation.

Corn on the cob – this will almost certainly block your woofer's intestine. The cob gets lodged in the small intestine, and if not removed by a vet can have fatal results.

Dairy products – dogs are lactose intolerant and can't digest milk or dairy foods properly.

Fat trimmings from meat – these are not good for dogs as they can cause pancreatitis.

Grapes and raisins – grapes contain a toxin that can cause liver damage and kidney failure.

Hops – can also be toxic to your dog.

Liver – in very small quantities this can be OK. It is high in vitamin A, but too much can affect a puppy's muscle and bone development.

Macadamia nuts – these contain a toxin that can cause terrible damage to pup's digestive, nervous and muscle systems.

Mushrooms and fungi – just as we have to take care to eat only certified edible mushrooms, dogs especially need watching on walks where the 'wrong' sort may grow.

 Onions and chives – in any form, these are among the very worst foods to give to dogs. They both contain disulfides and sulfoxides, which can cause anaemia and severely damage red blood cells.

 Persimmons, peaches and plums – if you have fruit trees that bear any of these fruits then do be aware that persimmon seeds and peach and plum pits can cause intestinal problems.

 Raw fish – resulting in a vitamin B deficiency, symptoms include loss of appetite, seizures and even death.

 Rhubarb and tomato leaves – these contain oxalates, which can adversely affect the dog's digestive, nervous and urinary systems.

Sugar in anything! – check ingredient labels thoroughly, but frankly giving your dog biscuits, cakes or indeed any sugar-rich treat is pretty daft. Obviously, just as with humans, too much sugar is not good for the system and can lead to canine dental problems, obesity and even diabetes.

 Yeast or dough – these will expand and rise in poor pup's tummy, causing painful – and smelly – gas and possibly leading to a rupture of the stomach and intestines.

Did you know?

According to research by the Pet Food Manufacturers Association (PMFA) the demand for complete dry dog food has increased by 90 per cent since 2004. Sales of dog treats have doubled, with the amount of moist dog food declining by almost a quarter and mixers by around a half.

CHAPTER 4

SHOWING OFF AND RECORD-BREAKERS

*Anybody who doesn't know what soap
tastes like never washed a dog.*

FRANKLIN P. JONES, AMERICAN REPORTER AND HUMORIST

Today our dogs' achievements are documented and celebrated via social and traditional media. From 'Best in Show' to the dog who can balance a stack of steaks on his nose, we humans love to watch our canine friends and to read about their talents. It is no coincidence, therefore, that dog shows are now such big business, well attended by people wanting to show their hounds, as well as those, in many cases non-dog owners, who simply want to enjoy the spectacle.

Dog shows and competitions

Bred to work, it wasn't until the middle of the 1800s that dogs began to be appreciated for their appearance and personalities rather than merely their strength or speed. In 1859, Setters and Pointers and their humans were invited to what is believed to be the first formal dog show in the world, held in Newcastle upon Tyne in northeast

England. Over the next decade there was a huge swell of popularity in the hobby of showing one's dog and the idea was quickly picked up in America. However, due to the Civil War, America didn't host its first dog show until 1877. Today dog shows take place all over the world, with some dogs travelling the globe in the manner of superstars as they collect piece after piece of silverware.

Crufts

One of the most famous dog shows in the world is Crufts, now held at the National Exhibition Centre in Birmingham. The brainchild of Charles Cruft, it is now one of the biggest and most prestigious dog events in the world. Much more than just a competition, Crufts today celebrates dogs in every conceivable sense – as workers, pedigrees, performers and more. A vast festival that attracts crowds of exhibitors and spectators, whether you are a wannabe dog owner, a dog lover or you take your dog to participate, Crufts is a paradise for all things canine. As well as all the classes and events it offers a great opportunity to talk to bodies like the Kennel Club Assured Breeders, rescue charities and breed experts. There are also masses of trade stands selling a dizzying array of barking bargains!

Crufts history

Leaving college in 1876, Charles Cruft accepted a job with James Spratt who had opened a shop in London selling his newly dreamed up confection: dog cakes.

In 1886 Cruft took over the management of the Allied Terrier Club Show at the Royal Aquarium in London, and in 1891 the first Crufts show was booked in to the Royal Agricultural Hall in Islington where there were an impressive 2,437 entries. The Kennel Club took over as organisers of Crufts in 1948 and the show was first televised in 1950. In 2000 Rescue Dog Agility was introduced to the programme, giving rescue dogs their well-deserved moment in the spotlight. The Best in Show prize has been awarded for the past 83 years, with 41 different breeds winning the sought-after title.

Did you know?

The very first organised Field Trial took place at Southill, Bedfordshire, in 1865. A sport that also quickly attracted a keen following among country gentlemen, this was probably the forerunner for the dog agility classes that have become so popular.

Crufts Best in Show winners since 2005

2015
Knopa – Scottish Terrier
2014
Afterglow Maverick Sabre – Standard Poodle
2013
Soletrader Peek A Boo – Petit Basset Griffon Vendéen
2012
Zentarr Elizabeth – Lhasa Apso
2011
The Kentuckian – Retriever (Flat Coated)
2010
Hungargunn Bear It'n Mind – Hungarian Vizsla
2009
Efbe's Hidalgo At Goodspice – Sealyham Terrier
2008
Philippe Olivier – Giant Schnauzer
2007
Fabulous Willy – Tibetan Terrier
2006
Caitland Isle Take a Chance – Australian Shepherd
2005
Cracknor Cause Celebre – Norfolk Terrier

Did you know?

The death of King George VI on 6 February 1952 threatened the possibility of the cancellation of Crufts. The show did go ahead, but two days later than originally scheduled.

Worldwide woofer shows

Crufts might be one of the most established and renowned dog shows in the world, but the World Dog Show is still considered by many as the pinnacle of the dog show schedule. The world's biggest dog show, on the last day of the event one lucky owner will see their hound crowned World's Best Dog. Held annually in one of the member countries of the Fédération Cynologique Internationale (FCI), more than 100 judges from 31 countries congregate to judge the dogs.

Other countries around the world hold their own major dog shows, including breed specific shows. Fun dog shows – or Companion Dog Shows to give them their correct name – are often found at the local fete or festival and are also universally popular, allowing family dogs and mutts to compete. In the UK at smaller shows classes such as Dog With the Waggiest Tail and Prettiest Bitch are run alongside sack races and basic dog agility.

Preparing to show your dog

Allow plenty of time to get to the show and to register your dog for the classes you wish to participate in. Registration may not be a quick process if the show is particularly busy.

Pack carefully, making sure to include grooming tools, dog treats and plenty of poo bags. A bowl and some water (although there is generally a water source available at shows) is essential and, if it is summertime, take a water-soaked towel in a cool bag in case your dog overheats and needs to lie down on a chilled surface.

When you register to compete you will be given a ring number. This needs to be worn in the ring, so take a pin with you in case the fastening on your number isn't secure.

Pay attention to the ring steward and listen carefully to any tannoy announcements. Classes will be called to the ring and you need to be entering the ring ready and calm, not flapping and panicking because you were chatting on your phone and missed the announcement.

Go to a few shows as a spectator before entering, as that way you'll know what is expected of you and your dog. Note how the judges look over the dogs and see if you can spot what they are looking for.

Enjoy it! Both you and your dog should find shows a pleasurable experience, but if you discover that it really doesn't suit you or your dog then don't push it. Showing is not for everyone. Whatever happens, remember to tell your dog that he is wonderful and that he will always be YOUR winner.

Go flying

Flyball is a team sport that first became popular in the USA. Catching on in the UK, it was first featured at Crufts in 1990. A fast-paced competition that will see your dog burning off energy and having a ball at the same time, two teams of four dogs compete at the same time, each using a parallel racing lane down which each dog runs in turn. Having to clear four hurdles in succession before triggering a pedal on the Flyball box, thus releasing a tennis ball, the dog must hold the ball before returning over the hurdles to the start line. The first team to have all dogs complete the course is declared the winner. Each dog must cross the finish line before the next dog can start. If a run is not completed correctly – if the dog drops the ball or misses a hurdle – the dog must re-run at the end of the line.

If you think your dog would enjoy and be good at Flyball, investigate groups in your area or keep an eye out at dog shows where Flyball teams often appear as a demonstration event.

Did you know?

In the USA there are annual Crazy Dog Grooming contests, featuring dogs with dyed fur and dressed up as characters, including Elvis and Yoda. The most bonkers designs can win dog owners up to US$5,000 in prize money.

What's yours called?

Registering a dog's show name is straightforward and can be done online at the Kennel Club's website. The Kennel Club's registration system records your puppy's birth and gives you the opportunity to give it a 'formal' name. No matter that you call it Rover or Bouncer at home, in the pedigree show ring your dog will be billed as whatever mouthful you bestow on the poor beast. The register can be cross referenced so that your show name is unique. If you want to compete at Crufts then your dog must be registered with the Kennel Club on the Breed Register. Dogs originating from other countries must have an Authority To Compete number before they are permitted to compete at any show. Dogs can start competing from six months of age.

Record-breaking dogs around the world

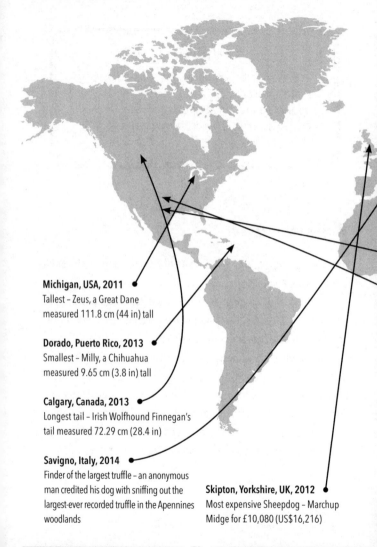

Michigan, USA, 2011
Tallest – Zeus, a Great Dane
measured 111.8 cm (44 in) tall

Dorado, Puerto Rico, 2013
Smallest – Milly, a Chihuahua
measured 9.65 cm (3.8 in) tall

Calgary, Canada, 2013
Longest tail – Irish Wolfhound Finnegan's
tail measured 72.29 cm (28.4 in)

Savigno, Italy, 2014
Finder of the largest truffle – an anonymous
man credited his dog with sniffing out the
largest-ever recorded truffle in the Apennines
woodlands

Skipton, Yorkshire, UK, 2012
Most expensive Sheepdog – Marchup
Midge for £10,080 (US$16,216)

Kaarst, Germany, 2013
Fastest dog to retrieve a person from water – Jack, a Newfoundland, covered 25 m (82 ft) in 1 minute 36.81 seconds

USA, 2013
Most treats balanced on a dog's nose – Monkey appeared on *Guinness World Records Unleashed* with 26 treats balanced on his nose

Shizuoka, Japan, 2013
The most dogs skipping on the same rope – no fewer than 14 dogs of Uchida Geinousha's Super Wan Wan Circus skipped on a rope in a televised record attempt

Texas, USA, 2003
Most tennis balls held in the mouth by a dog – Augie, a Golden Retriever, gathered up and held five tennis balls in his chops

Adelaide, Australia, 2012
The loudest bark – measuring 113.1 dB, Golden Retriever Charlie was recorded during a 'Bark in the Park' event

Record-breaking births

Being a record breaker must have been of small comfort to Tia, a Neapolitan Mastiff, back in 2004. Producing 24 pups, the largest ever recorded litter, on 29 November 2004 the big momma gave birth to nine females and 15 males. Born by Caesarean section, sadly one was stillborn and three died in the first week. In December 2014 Keeler the Dobermann surprised her owner Zara Hayes from Nottinghamshire, UK, by delivering a litter of 14 bundles of squirmy joy – a British record for a Dobermann litter – just in time for Christmas. Buying Keeler who was advertised for sale as 'possibly being pregnant', the shocked but nevertheless delighted Mrs Hayes is reported as being stunned when they saw the sixth puppy emerge. One can only speculate on how she must have felt by the time Keeler produced puppy number 14.

Biggest and smallest canine buddies

When Digby the Chihuahua was brought into the Southbridge RSPCA centre in 2015 he immediately found a friend. And although he had to jump up onto a chair in order to be nose-to-nose with his new pal, he and Nero – a 58-kilogram (130-pound) Mastiff – quickly became inseparable. Looking like his small buddy's minder, and proving that his heart is as big as he is, Nero keeps a watchful eye on the poor little pup, who was found hiding behind bins in north London.

Did you know?

During the Bulldog Rescue & Rehoming Trust's annual Bulldog Picnic in 2014 an attempt was made to break the record for the number of Bulldogs in one place at the same time. The current record stands at 312 (dating back to the Bulldog Club Incorporated 1975 centenary show), but alas the attempt fell short with just 267 present at the event in Lavant, West Sussex. To join in with the next attempt, visit www. bulldogrescue.org.uk.

Most unlikely canine buddies

When Manni the wild boar piglet was found in a field in southwest Germany he was frightened and hungry. Taken home by the Dahlhaus family, their pet Jack Russell Terrier Candy took an instant liking to the little piggy, which was reciprocated by Manni. The pair quickly established a firm and affectionate bond.

Similarly, there have been reports of unlikely friendships springing up between dogs and elephants, orangutans, lion cubs and even, as is the case with Roo and Penny, chickens. Roo the two-legged Chihuahua from Georgia, USA, not only uses a specially adapted wheelchair to get around, but his best friend Penny just happens to be a chicken. Just nine weeks old when Alicia Williams saved her from a laboratory, Penny is a Silky, a breed well known for its fine and soft feathers. Her saviour worked at an animal hospital, where Penny was given sanctuary. Roo was a baby – only seven weeks old – when he was found abandoned in a park. His front legs were not properly developed and so a wheelchair was designed and fitted to the pup to enable Roo to get about. Meeting Penny, the two immediately struck up a firm if unusual friendship – one that has turned them into an internet sensation.

CHAPTER 5

WORK LIKE A DOG

They usually bark when there is a stranger about,
but it is an expression of unmitigated joy.

AUTHOR NORMAN STRUNG ON HOW LABRADORS MAKE VERY FRIENDLY WATCHDOGS

Dogs have worked with and for man for centuries in a wide variety of roles. Using strength, stamina, intelligence and, of course, their incredible sense of smell, their natural talents have been – and continue to be – well utilised.

Did you know?

Shepherds and farmers have used dogs for many years to herd sheep and cattle and other animals. It inspired a television show, One Man and His Dog, *in which Sheepdogs competed. The show ran for 23 years on the BBC until 2013, when it was incorporated into* Countryfile.

Friends, Romans...

Our canine friends have long been used as workers. In domestic service 'turnspit dogs' were used to turn a treadmill that was linked to a roasting spit or to a butter-churning can, while the ancient Greeks used to breed a Mastiff-like dog, which they used as a highly efficient protection officer. The Greeks also bred a hound dog for hunting hares, which they trained to track and then drive the quarry into traps. The Romans used Mastiffs in their gladiatorial shows and called their breed Molossus. An aggressive fighting dog, it came as some surprise to the Romans when, on arrival in England, they discovered that the British Mastiff was even bigger and fiercer than theirs. The Romans also employed dogs to hunt and guard homes and livestock.

Prayer pups and hard hounds

When the Barbarians trashed the Roman Empire they brought with them dogs like the Tibetan Prayer Dog (now better known as the Tibetan Spaniel). Trained to turn the prayer wheel in monasteries, monks wrote prayers on parchments and placed them in the revolving box. The theory was that as the wheel revolved the prayers were being constantly 'said'. Also used as a watchdog, a lesser-known job of these dogs was as hand warmers. The monks would sit on the floor with their legs crossed and their hands folded inside the sleeves of their robes, in which nestled a nice cosy little dog! Less lap and more scrap, the Normans brought the Bloodhound with them when they invaded England. A superb sniffer dog that was a real asset to hunters, the Bloodhound was also used in battle – often wearing as much armour as the human soldiers.

Dog slog

> *When an eighty-five pound mammal licks your tears away,*
> *then tries to sit on your lap, it's hard to feel sad.*
>
> KRISTAN HIGGINS, AUTHOR OF *CATCH OF THE DAY*

In more modern times dogs have been, and continue to be, used in therapy for people suffering with depression, anger management issues and chronic illnesses. In clinical settings dogs are used to comfort the terminally ill, and as assistants they provide invaluable support to those with impaired sight, hearing and mobility. Employed in farming, sled pulling, rescue missions, in warfare, policing and on country estates (by retrieving fowl and fish) man's best friend is no shirker when it comes to hard work.

A nose for it

A dog has an incredible sense of smell and taste, with some breeds boasting 'super snouts' that are invaluable in police work for the locating of drugs. The charity Medical Detection Dogs (www.medicaldetectiondogs.org.uk) works with researchers, NHS trusts and universities to help train dogs to recognise the odours of human diseases such as cancer and diabetes. Support Dogs (www.supportdogs.org.uk) train dogs to assist those suffering with epilepsy, the most common neurological illness. Many sufferers are unable to control their seizures through medication and are constantly fearful that a seizure will strike at any time, which has a hugely limiting effect on their lives. Seizure alert dogs are trained to provide a 100 per cent reliable warning up to 50 minutes prior to a seizure occurring, giving their owners time to find a place of safety and privacy before the seizure strikes.

Konnie's nose for trouble

Konrad (Konnie to his loving family), a Standard Poodle, had a talent for sniffing out problems. Owner Kate recalls:

The first time we noticed his gift was when my daughter had had a C-section. She had been home from hospital for about a week when one morning Konnie walked up to her chair and pushed his nose into her lap. He kept doing this all day, which had us rattled as it was totally out of character. By the evening he was really shoving his nose at my daughter's 'nether regions' and at the same time she began to feel unwell. A few hours later her temperature was seriously raised and the doctor ordered an ambulance. It was discovered that she had developed an internal infection as a result of her Caesarean. She stayed in hospital for over a week. We put Konnie's behaviour down to coincidence but then a month later he started hassling our elderly Pug-cross bitch. She had been spayed and Konnie had never troubled her before, but now he kept nudging her rear end. One day she rolled on to her back and to my horror there was a large swelling. It turned out to be a mammary tumour. It was removed and Konnie didn't bother her again until some months later. When he started again, this time I looked and the tumour was back! Another time he followed a dog in the forest. I asked the owner if the dog was OK then she said the dog had just been diagnosed with diabetes. Then there was a three-legged greyhound who had lost her leg after a hit and run. Konnie started sniffing her amputation site so I asked her owner if she was OK. She said she was but got her checked out anyway – and lo and behold the dog had an infection.

Did you know?

Used by monks to help find lost or stranded travellers in the Alps, St Bernard dogs were originally called hospice dogs because they assisted at the Great St Bernard Hospice. Over time, however, they became known by the name of the monastery.

Disability dogs

The UK charity Canine Partners does incredible work, training dogs to act as the limbs of disabled people. Founded in 1990 by dog welfare campaigner Anne Conway and vet Liz Ormerod, Canine Partners was the result of these ladies' research into assistance dog programmes around the world. Based on the model of The SOHO Foundation of Holland, an established assistance dog's programme, and with similar organisations elsewhere in the world, dogs are trained to do everything from picking up dropped items to unloading washing machines. Dogs can also help their owners to get undressed, open doors and hand money or cards to cashiers in shops. Obviously 'cleaning up' after a dog when you are out and about is not an option for a disabled person, so all Canine Partner dogs are trained to go to the toilet on command, enabling the disabled person to establish a designated dog loo area in his or her own garden. From soldiers who have lost the use of their limbs in war to those with long-term disabilities, a Canine Partner can transform the quality of a person's life.

Guide dogs

The first organised attempt to train guide dogs was at a hospital for the blind in Paris in 1780. In 1788, Josef Riesinger, a blind sieve-maker from Vienna, trained a Spitz so effectively that people sometimes questioned whether he was genuinely blind.

Modern guide dogs date back to World War One, when numerous soldiers returned from the front blinded, often by poison gas. A German doctor, Dr Gerhard Stalling, had the idea of training dogs to help 'guide' these unfortunate men. Dr Stalling opened the world's first guide dog school for the blind in Oldenburg in 1916.

In the 1920s, an American Dorothy Harrison Eustis began training dogs for the army, police and customs service in Switzerland and it was Eustis who launched the guide dog movement internationally. Setting up guide dog schools in Switzerland and the USA, she named the schools the Seeing Eye. In 1930 after hearing about the Seeing Eye, two British women, Muriel Crooke and Rosamund Bond, contacted Eustis, who dispatched one of her trainers to the UK. In 1934 the two British women founded The Guide Dogs for the Blind Association. Since then guide dog schools have opened all around the world.

> **Did you know?**
>
> An early suggestion of guide dogs is depicted in art. Uncovering a mural buried amid the ruins of ancient Herculaneum, Italy, archaeologists saw featured in the picture a dog clearly leading a blind man.

When you and your beloved dog rely on each other for nearly everything, your love is multiplied to epic proportions.

DIANNE PHELPS, UNSIGHTED, WHO HAS HAD SEVEN GUIDE DOGS

Hearing dogs

Dogs can also be trained to alert deaf people to various sounds and danger signals, and in so doing provide a life-changing level of independence, confidence and companionship. The charity Hearing Dogs for Deaf People came about after Professor Lee Bustad, Dean of the School of Veterinary Medicine at Washington State University, included reference to the training of dogs to assist deaf people in the USA in a speech he gave at the British Small Animal Veterinary Association International Symposium in 1979. Dr Bruce Fogle, a vet present at the conference, was immediately interested in learning more. He contacted the Royal National Institute for the Deaf (now named Action on Hearing Loss) and in 1981 Fogle and Lady Wright from the National Institute succeeded in piloting a scheme in the UK. The scheme was officially launched in February 1982 at Crufts Dog Show in London.

An 'out of this world' mongrel

Stray mongrels were used in all sorts of horrible experiments in the past, and sadly still are today in some quarters. In 1957, a stray mongrel called Laika was selected by scientists in the Soviet Union who wanted to conduct a very particular experiment: to confirm their belief that organisms from Earth could survive in space.

To prove their theory they sent the world's second artificial space satellite, *Sputnik 2*, into space with Laika on board. Attached to a life-support system, it was reported that Laika suffered no ill effects, even at an altitude of 3,200 kilometres (2,000 miles), but tragically her life-support system ran out of batteries just a couple of days into her incredible journey. However, a report in 2002 suggested that she died from overheating and panic only hours after the mission began. The new evidence was presented at a World Space Congress in Houston, Texas, USA, by Dimitri Malashenkov of the Institute for Biological Problems in Moscow.

A monument honouring fallen cosmonauts was erected in 1997 at Star City on the outskirts of Moscow. Laika, quite rightly, is featured with her fellow space travellers.

Did you know?

Gareth Wyn Jones, a Welsh hill farmer, attached a camera to the collar of his Border Collie, Cap, and turned him into a YouTube sensation. Capturing Cap rounding up sheep, the clip has been watched all over the world by more than 30,000 viewers.

Hot spots

English aristocrats during the early 1700s were among the first known to use Dalmatians to accompany their carriages. Dalmatians often ran in pairs, one on either side of the coach, offering an effective deterrent to highwaymen and conferring something of a social status. Later, these speedy spotty dogs were employed by firefighters. Happy to run with horses when a fire alarm rang, the Dalmatians would bark to alert those nearby that the fire wagon was about to come out of the fire station. Running alongside the horse-drawn vehicle the dogs stood guard over the wagon, horses and firefighter's belongings while the fire was dealt with. Many stations in the USA and the UK adopted the Dalmatian as a mascot even when vehicles were no longer horse drawn, keeping one in residence to see off rats and mice. Today the Dalmatian remains the breed that is associated with fire services.

During World War One dogs were used to locate the wounded on the battlefield and today dogs, including mutts, are trained to find and rescue people in disaster situations, such as earthquakes and floods, saving lives that otherwise would almost certainly be lost. There are even dogs in Italy today being taught to become canine lifeguards by going to the aid of swimmers who have got into difficulty.

CHAPTER 6

DOGS IN SPORT

I see you stand like greyhounds in the slips,
Straining upon the start. The game's afoot:
Follow your spirit; and upon this charge,
Cry 'God for Harry! England! and Saint George!'

WILLIAM SHAKESPEARE, *HENRY V*

Greyhounds and Huskies are known for their speed and strength, while scent following is becoming increasingly popular as a competitive sport for dogs of all breeds. In all three instances dogs get to run at their maximum speed, although the potential for (human) financial gain is greater and indeed contentious when it comes to Greyhound racing.

Greyhound racing

Just as horse racing divides opinion, with some believing it is cruel, the same applies to the racing of Greyhounds. Certainly when it began the sport left a great deal to be desired in terms of the dogs' welfare, but there have been significant strides in improvement and while the is-it-cruel-or-not debate still rages, it is generally agreed that matters are far better managed and monitored now. In 1979 the British Greyhound Racing Board was set up to promote and improve the Greyhound racing industry, and to consult with the National Greyhound Racing Club (NGRC) on matters including the rules of racing and how to improve the care and welfare of racing dogs. In 2009 the Greyhound Board of Great Britain (GBGB) was launched, taking on the functions of both the British Greyhound Racing Board and the National Greyhound Racing Club. The sport now spends approximately one third of its annual budget on welfare – in excess of £4,000,000 – investing in aspects of racing including track safety, kennel conditions and the welfare of retired Greyhounds. The GBGB also works closely with major welfare charities via the Greyhound Knowledge Forum. Representatives include the RSPCA, Blue Cross and Dogs Trust. And whether you love or loathe Greyhound racing (and if it's the latter then there are certainly organisations that lobby against it that you can add your voice to), what cannot be ignored is the rich history of Greyhound racing and some of its incredible champions.

You may know a gentleman by his horse,
his hawk and his greyhound.

OLD WELSH PROVERB

The start of the race

A sport enjoyed by many, Greyhound racing as we know it today was brought to Britain by American Owen Patrick Smith, inventor of the first mechanical lure and oval, rather than straight, track in the US. Immediately seeing the potential for international appeal, Smith and his colleagues set up the Greyhound Racing Association (GRA) and promptly built and opened the Belle Vue Greyhound Racing Stadium in Gorton, Manchester, in 1926. At the inaugural meeting in July of that year 1,700 people watched six races. Word of mouth was positive and before long numbers swelled, with crowds of 11,000 attending meetings.

Stadiums across the country began springing up, with London's White City, originally built for the 1908 Olympic Games, turned into a Greyhound racetrack. In 1927 White City hosted the first English Greyhound Derby, offering a staggering prize of £1,000. The Derby remains the highlight of the Greyhound racing calendar and is today held at Wimbledon Stadium.

Greyhound racing enjoyed swift-growing popularity, dipping for the first time during the years of World War Two. A second slump occurred when live horse racing began being broadcast on television, further compounded by a property slump in the 1970s. Today there are 26 tracks in England and Scotland, with the sport still attracting racegoers of all ages.

Did you know?

To curtail foul play, in 1928 rules for racing were dictated through the newly set up National Greyhound Racing Club. This meant that vets checked that dogs were fit to race and had not been doped or nobbled in any way, with the organisation updating the rules annually. All tracks and individuals had to be licensed by the club, and by 1928 all dogs had to have passports or identity books. These are still used today.

A four (long) legged friend?

You might be forgiven for discounting a retired racing Greyhound when contemplating a dog, but according to the Retired Greyhound Trust (RGT), an organisation established in 1975 and which has since found homes for over 60,000 dogs, Greyhounds make excellent pets. Fortunately the misconceptions associated with the breed have been well documented over the past decade, leading to a surge in their popularity as pets, but in case you need any convincing…

Temperament? Naturally very calm, gentle and self-possessed, these mild-mannered souls are one of the world's oldest breeds and so are genuine thoroughbreds. They make excellent companions for humans and are usually very good with children.

Good with other pets? Retired Greyhounds may find it difficult to throw off the instinct to give chase to anything small and furry. If you have a cat, bunny or other small fluffy creature make sure you check whether or not the Greyhound in question has a tendency to regress to its track mentality.

Dog or bitch? The differences tend to be less pronounced than in many other breeds. Spaying or castrating can normally alleviate any behavioural problems and is recommended.

Long legs mean long walks? No! Just 20 minutes twice daily will generally be perfectly adequate for most Greyhounds. Remember, these dogs are sprinters not marathon runners and as such they use up their energy in short bursts. The rest of the time they are very fond of snoozing. Besides, by the time they retire from the track they are past their physical prime and really don't need or want to go for very long runs.

Long legs mean a big bed? Again, no! Fold an old quilt in half and that will do nicely. A word of caution, however; Greyhounds like to stretch out and a sofa or bed will be especially appealing to them. Be prepared to stand firm if you have a 'no dogs on the furniture' rule.

If dog ownership isn't something that your lifestyle could accommodate the RGT has over 70 branches across the UK, from the Isle of Skye to Jersey. Volunteers for dog walks and to help raise funds are always welcome – the perfect way to enjoy some canine companionship! And if Greyhounds aren't your preferred breed there are many other dog charities all over the world that also welcome volunteers.

A speedy stud

A Greyhound that smashed a Sydney track record to win its first race start was retired to stud because he could earn more money off the track. In April 2014 Shakey Jakey took a phenomenal 22-length lead to win the sixth race at Sydney's Wentworth Park. An offer of AUS$700,000 was made to owner David Pringle, topped by a second offer of AUS$1,000,000, but canny Pringle refused both. Instead he decided to retire Shakey Jakey to stud, which has since seen him amassing a fortune in stud fees.

Did you know?

In 1925 Balto the Siberian Husky led a team of Huskies on the final leg to deliver a precious cargo of diphtheria serum. Travelling over 960 kilometres (600 miles), teams of these wonderful dogs raced from Anchorage to epidemic-ridden Nome. A statue of Balto stands in New York's Central Park to commemorate the Nome serum run and bears the inscription 'Endurance, Fidelity, Intelligence'. The Iditarod Trail Race was launched in the 1970s and is held annually in March in memory of the great serum run.

MUSH!

Sled dogs have been 'on the pull' for some 4,000 years. As well as needing dogs for protection and hunting, those in the frozen north depended on dogs for transport. Great explorers like Amundsen, Peary and Byrd would never have made it to the icy wildernesses of the polar regions without sled dogs, who have also played a key part in the civilisation of the world's snowbound zones. These splendid creatures also assisted in both world wars and by 1873 were working with the Canadian Mounties.

The race is on!

Starting from Winnipeg, Manitoba, and finishing in St Paul, Minnesota, the first established sled dog race is recorded as having taken place in 1850 (although it is likely that informal racing was commonplace before then). Growing in popularity, sled dog racing now takes place all over the world – even in places where snow is as rare as purple-spotted Dalmatians. If you live in the UK then the Siberian Husky Club of Great Britain is a great place to start if you're keen to find out more about competing or spectating. The club's Aviemore Sled Dog Rally is the longest running and largest event of its kind in the UK, which while somewhat ambitious for a newcomer to the sport, attracts over 200 teams each year. Suitable for all ages, there is even a competition for juniors.

British sled dog races usually take place on a woodland or forest circuit. Teams start racing at timed intervals and are divided into classes based on the number of dogs in the team.

Sled dog race classes

𝔸 - no more than 8 dogs, no less than 5

𝔹 - no more than 6 dogs, no less than 4

ℂ - no more than 4 dogs, no less than 3

𝔻 - 2 dogs only

𝔼 - no more than 3 dogs, no less than 2

𝕌 - unlimited, no less than 5 dogs

Junior 1 - 1 dog (dog 1 year+/driver 12–15)

Junior 2 - 1-2 dogs (dog 1 year+/driver 8–11)

Cani-Cross - 1 dog and a competitor, racing on foot

Bike-Joring - 1 dog and a driver pedalling on a bicycle

Scooter 1 - 1 dog and a driver riding a two-wheeled scooter

Did you know?

The Disney film Iron Will *features the 1917 version of the Winnipeg to St Paul race, which was won by Albert Campbell, a Métis from Pas, Manitoba.*

Scent tracking

A dog sport that sees dogs picking up on a scent and following it across a terrain to an ultimate target, scent tracking is gaining in popularity all over the world. A fun element of training that is usually given to help dogs become search or search-and-rescue workers, a defined track has a starting point in an open space. The dogs are given a scent to follow from a person who has walked the course before the dogs arrive . The competing dogs then race, often over obstacles such as fences, hills and streams, to locate an object or target at the end of the track. Information on tracking trials in your local area should be available from local dog-focused organisations and from national bodies such as the Kennel Club.

Did you know?

In Australia tracking is a popular recreational sport for many dogs and their owners. All types of dogs complete in tracking trials, from toy breeds to larger dogs like Rottweilers.

CHAPTER 7

DOGS IN ART

If you eliminate smoking and gambling, you will be amazed to find that almost all an Englishman's pleasures can be, and mostly are, shared by his dog.

GEORGE BERNARD SHAW, PLAYWRIGHT

The favourite choice of subject of many famous artists down the ages, critically acclaimed art that features dogs hang in galleries all over the world. From American artist Cassius Marcellus Coolidge's famous dogs playing poker to Edouard Manet's *A King Charles Spaniel*, one in a series of dog portraits by the Impressionist, canine-inspired painting is a trend that has endured. On greetings cards, jigsaw puzzles, place mats, calendars and in advertising, dogs remain a hugely popular image. Indeed *Dogs Playing Poker* was a series of paintings created by Cassius Marcellus Coolidge when he was commissioned to come up with an advertising campaign for cigars. Two of these paintings later sold for just under US$6,000,000. You could say that this was 'a pair' that saw the artist enjoying a 'straight flush' in terms of success.

> ### *Did you know?*
>
> *Touring Japan in 1937, Helen Keller, author, activist and the first deaf-blind person to earn a bachelor's degree, was given an Akita, which she asked for having heard the story of Hachikō.*

Ando's Hachikō

A sculpture of an Akita called Hachikō by Japanese sculptor Takeshi Ando stands in Tokyo's Shibuya train station. In the 1920s Hachikō would see his master off to work at the station every morning, returning to collect him at the end of the day. When his owner died in 1925 Hachikō refused to leave the station, waiting in vain for his master to come home. Regular passengers soon realised what was happening and they began to bring food for Hachikō. News of his incredible loyalty spread far and wide and in 1934 a statue of Hachikō was erected at the station, where by now the dog had been waiting for the professor for almost ten years. When he died in 1935 Hachikō's bones were laid to rest next to his master's grave. With the outbreak of World War Two and metal now a precious commodity, Hachikō's statue was melted down in order to make arms. However, after the war a group of Hachikō fans had another commissioned from the son of the original sculptor. Erected in 1948, the memorial to this loyal Akita stands proudly once more.

Bobby, Canem and the piddler

Other notable statues of dogs include a memorial to the dog known as Greyfriars Bobby. In 1858 John Gray was buried in old Greyfriars Churchyard in Edinburgh, Scotland. His dog Bobby, a Skye Terrier, is said to have slept on his master's grave for the following 14 years until his own death – a tale of such loyalty that a statue was the least the little dog deserved.

Meanwhile the Canary Islands proudly display a statue of the rare breed of dog, called *Canem* in Latin, after which the islands are named. Cast in bronze and lolling on a plinth in Las Palmas, the dog reminds people that the Canaries are in fact named after dogs rather than birds. And over in Brussels a companion statue to the urinating boy called *Manneken Pis*, first seen in the early seventeenth century, is *Zinneke Pis*. A dog cocking his leg on a bollard may not be considered 'art' by the critics, but he certainly makes it into thousands of holiday snaps.

Did you know?

The Kennel Club Dog Art Gallery in London houses the largest collection of dog paintings in Europe. It is open Monday to Friday by appointment. For more information, visit www.thekennelclub.org.uk/our-resource.

*Know yourself. Don't accept your dog's admiration as
conclusive evidence that you are wonderful.*

ASK ANN LANDERS, *CHICAGO SUN-TIMES* ADVICE COLUMN

Old masters

Artist Pierre-Auguste Renoir (1841–1919) often featured small dogs
in his works. These include *Madame Renoir with a Dog*, which was
painted in1880. Another famous painting that includes a canine
subject is *The Arnolfini Portrait*. Painted by Netherlandish artist Jan
van Eyck (1390–1441) and hanging in London's National Gallery, the
scene is of a wedding between an Italian merchant and a colleague's
daughter. At their feet is a small Terrier. The dog is said to symbolise
fidelity, companionship and love. If you look carefully you can also
see the artist in the picture – he included himself in the background,
reflected in the mirror, as a painter creating the subject's portrait!

Did you know?

*During the Renaissance, detailed portraits of the
dog as a symbol of fidelity and loyalty appeared
in mythological, allegorical and religious art
throughout Europe and could be found on the
easels of Jan van Eyck, Leonardo da Vinci, Albrecht
Dürer and Diego Velázquez.*

Picasso's Lump

Believed by many to be the greatest and most influential artist of the twentieth century, Pablo Picasso was born in Spain in 1881. A painter, sculptor, printmaker, ceramicist and theatrical set designer, he was the co-founder of the Cubist movement, as well as a pioneer of several other styles. He was also devoted to his dog, a Dachshund called Lump. The dog originally belonged to photographer David Douglas Duncan, but when the pooch met Picasso in 1957 the match was one made in heaven. Allowing Lump access all areas, including his studio, the great artist featured his beloved dog in more than 15 of his works. A partnership for 16 years, master and dog died within weeks of each other.

Did you know?

The dog was regularly featured in Greek art. Cerberus, the three-headed hound guarding the entrance to hell, and the hunting dogs that accompanied the virgin goddess of the chase, Diana, were all depicted in various art forms.

Did you know?

Many portraits in the Royal Collection, which is held in trust for the UK by Queen Elizabeth II, depict dogs and their regal owners, with some pets even captured on canvas or in sculpture alone. After his death, a life-size marble statue of Noble, Queen Victoria's beloved Collie, was sculpted by Princess Louise, Queen Victoria's daughter, and now stands in Osborne House on the Isle of Wight.

What the Dickens?!

Having adopted a rescue dog, photographer Dan Bannino was inspired to embark on an artistic project that entailed using models from a local dog shelter. *Poetic Dogs* entailed four months' work based at the shelter, learning about his subjects and trying to figure out how to transform the dogs into his favourite authors. The dogs were untrained, fearful and completely inexperienced as models, so Bannino had to ditch his camera flash and stuff his pockets full of dog treats in order to secure canine cooperation. Costuming the dogs came next, and then much waiting around, poised to snap the exact expressions he needed. View the incredible photographs, including canine equivalents of Charles Dickens, Edith Sitwell, Ernest Hemingway, Leo Tolstoy and Mark Twain, at www.danbannino.com.

CHAPTER 8

DOGS IN LITERATURE

Bullseye in *Oliver Twist*, Pilot in *Jane Eyre*, Scamper in *The Secret Seven*, a whole host of canine characters in the novels of Jilly Cooper – dogs are often featured in books, and are sometimes integral to the plot. As for poetry, their antics and characters have been well used as subject matter.

Tom's Little Dog

Tom told his dog called Tim to beg,
And up at once he sat,
His two clear amber eyes fixed fast,
His haunches on his mat.
Tom poised a lump of sugar on
His nose; then, 'Trust!' says he;
Stiff as a guardsman sat his Tim;
Never a hair stirred he.

'Paid for!' says Tom; and in a trice
Up jerked that moist black nose;
A snap of teeth, a crunch, a munch,
And down the sugar goes!

WALTER DE LA MARE

Often cast in great works of literature and in popular books today, dogs have inspired novelists, playwrights and poets for thousands of years. It is believed that the first author of canine literature was a Roman scholar called Marcus Terentius Varro (116–27 BCE); a philosopher who wrote extensively on many different subjects, including agriculture. In his work *Des Rustica (Farm Topics)* he proffers advice on different breeds, canine diet and even pointers on training.

Did you know?

In the King James Bible, dogs are mentioned on 14 occasions. The only dog mentioned by specific breed is the Greyhound, which occurs in Proverbs 30:29–31.

There be three things which go well, yea, four are comely in going:
A lion, which is strongest among beasts, and turneth not away for any;
A greyhound; an he-goat also; and a king…

Dogs were given starring roles in early fables such as Aesop's *The Dog and the Shadow*, from which the reader learns that being greedy and clutching at shadows is not a sensible way of conducting oneself. Shakespeare also makes mention of dogs, although it is only in *The Two Gentlemen of Verona* that a dog gets anything approaching a decent role (the cheeky mongrel Crab, who belongs to the servant Launce). Some other breeds that do at least get a shout-out from the Bard include Greyhounds (*Henry V*); Spaniels (*Antony and Cleopatra*); Greyhounds, mongrels and Spaniels (*Macbeth*); and Hounds (*A Midsummer Night's Dream*).

In the past two hundred years we have also seen dogs cropping up in the works of great writers like Charles Dickens. Who can fail to feel at least a degree of pity for the poor terrier Bullseye, the dog belonging to bully boy Bill Sikes in *Oliver Twist*? Treated appallingly by Sikes, Dickens describes the dog as vicious but keeps him loyal to Bill and his aggressive and thieving ways, right to the bitter end. It perhaps suggests that the great writer knew something of the loyalty of a canine friend?

In *Memoirs from the House of the Dead*, Fyodor Dostoyevsky paints an evocative portrait of prison life, aided by the detailed conversations between himself and the prison dog, a confidante whose presence evidently provided considerable comfort.

> *A great dog, whose black and white colour made him a distinct object against the trees… a lion-like creature with long hair and a huge head.*
>
> JANE EYRE, ON MEETING PILOT, MR ROCHESTER'S DOG, FOR THE FIRST TIME IN *JANE EYRE* BY CHARLOTTE BRONTË

Ten books for children starring dogs

Clifford the Big Red Dog
by Norman Bridwell

Dip the Puppy
by Spike Milligan

*Hairy Maclary from
Donaldson's Dairy*
by Lynley Dodd

Harry Potter series
(in which Fang, Hagrid's dog, appears)
by J. K. Rowling

Kipper the Dog series
by Mick Inkpen

Spot the Dog series
by Eric Hill

The Hundred and One Dalmatians
by Dodie Smith

*The Tale Of Samuel Whiskers or
The Roly-Poly Pudding*
(John Joiner is the Terrier that
foils the rats' plan to turn Tom
Kitten into a pudding)
by Beatrix Potter

The Wizard of Oz
(Toto belonging to Dorothy)
by L. Frank Baum

Walter the Farting Dog
by William Kotzwinkle
and Glenn Murray

Dogs in the nursery

Frequently used as characters in children's literature, one of the most famous of these is Nana the dog, the Newfoundland belonging to the Darling family in *Peter Pan* by J. M. Barrie. Said to have been inspired by Barrie's own dog, Nana howled her shaggy head off in a bid to alert the Darling parents that their children were absconding with Peter. In the book, Mr Darling is then so mortified that he has ignored their faithful friend's warning siren that he takes it upon himself to sleep in her kennel in her place until his children are safely returned.

Enid Blyton's *The Famous Five* and *The Secret Seven* books include dogs Timmy and Scamper respectively. Both pets to the groups of young adventurers, who always seem to be embroiled in a mystery, the dogs inevitably play their parts in bringing down criminals and baddies.

Did you know?

The term 'dog days of summer' was coined by the ancient Greeks and Romans but has endured to this day. For the ancients, the term referred to the rising of the 'Dog Star', Sirius, which coincided with the hottest days of summer.

Very curious

The investigation into the murder of Wellington, a Poodle, by a young autistic teenager seems perhaps an unlikely premise for a bestseller but The Curious Incident of the Dog in the Night-time *by Mark Haddon was a smash hit, not just as a book but also as a stage adaptation which plays to packed houses in London's West End and on Broadway.*

Fidos of contemporary fiction

Cyril, Angus's dog with the gold tooth and a taste for beer, appears in Alexander McCall Smith's *44 Scotland Street* series, while in Jilly Cooper's Rutshire-based books dogs get significant roles and fabulous names. A self-confessed dog lover, Cooper's animal characters even get their own billing at the front of each book; a cast list that is essential given the number of characters in each of her enormous – and enormously enjoyable – books. But arguably the most significant and famous doggy story of all time is Sheila Burnford's 1961 novel *The Incredible Journey*. Later given the Disney treatment (1963), this is the tear-jerking story of a Labrador, a Bull Terrier and a Siamese cat stranded hundreds of kilometres from home. Determined to make the journey across the Canadian wilderness and back to the bosom of their family, this glorious tale of courage and determination is a literary tribute to the qualities of intelligence, loyalty, tenacity and resourcefulness – qualities that dogs have in buckets.

Ten dogs and their literary owners

Quinine (Dachshund) and Anton Chekhov

Wessex (Terrier) and Thomas Hardy

Boatswain (Newfoundland) and Lord Byron

Cliché (Poodle) and Dorothy Parker

Bluebell (Greyhound) and Jilly Cooper

Chopper (Jack Russell) and Roald Dahl

Peter (Wire-haired Terrier) and Agatha Christie

Charley (Poodle) and John Steinbeck

Pongo (Pug) and Donna Tartt

Sapphire (Greyhound) and J. K. Rowling

Rovers of rhyme

> *All in the town were still asleep,*
> *When the sun came up with a shout and a leap.*
> *In the lonely streets unseen by man,*
> *A little dog danced. And the day began.*
>
> RUPERT BROOKE, FROM 'THE LITTLE DOG'S DAY'

Poetry about dogs has delighted us for generations. In anthologies all over the world you will find poems about different breeds, pet dogs, fierce dogs and even lyrical prayers for deceased dogs. One of the most famous pup poems is Elizabeth Barrett Browning's 'To Flush, My Dog'. A leading and prolific poet of the Victorian age, Browning is said to have loved Flush dearly and taken great comfort from his presence during her long-term poor health.

> *And this dog was satisfied,*
> *If a pale thin hand would glide,*
> *Down his dewlaps sloping, -*
> *Which he pushed his nose within,*
> *After, - platforming his chin*
> *On the palm left open.*
>
> ELIZABETH BARRETT BROWNING, FROM 'TO FLUSH, MY DOG'
> **Friend or foe?**

Hark! hark! the dogs do bark,
The beggars are coming to town.
Some in rags, and some in tags,
And some in velvet gowns.

Dating back to thirteenth-century England, this rhyme explains how communities used dogs to warn them that strangers were approaching. During this period in history beggars and minstrels travelled around and often included coded messages of rebellion in their performances and recitals. Passing gossip and propaganda to the common people in lyrics and rhymes led to devious plots and uprisings against those in power and so all incoming visitors were regarded with suspicion even if they were wearing 'velvet gowns'.

CHAPTER 9

DOGS IN MUSIC

Where there are dogs and music, people have a good time.
EMMYLOU HARRIS, SINGER AND SONGWRITER

As with art and literature, dogs have moved musicians and lyricists to write and record songs that pay homage to man's and woman's best friend. And in one instance a dog-loving super group even recorded a secret message for dogs on one of their album tracks. Sir Paul McCartney has admitted that on The Beatles' *Sgt. Pepper's Lonely Hearts Club Band* album, recorded in 1967, they included a recording of an ultrasonic whistle, a sound that only dogs can hear. It is found in the track 'A Day in the Life'; dig out your copy and give your hound a musical message.

How much of a hit?

A popular novelty song that has endured is 'How Much is That Doggie in the Window?' Written by Bob Merrill in 1952, the original version was recorded in the USA by Patti Page and released in January 1953 by Mercury Records. It reached number one on both the *Billboard* and *Cash Box* magazine charts and sold in excess of two million copies. Because of distribution problems it had to be re-recorded for the UK but even so it was a hit, making Lita Roza the first British female to go to number one in the hit parade (it was also the first number one with a question in its title!). The song entered the charts in March 1953 at number nine and then spent 11 weeks in the charts, reaching number one in April.

Did you know?

A woman reported sleepless nights over a three-year period after being beleaguered by a rare illness involving the song 'How Much is That Doggie in the Window?' According to a report in The Telegraph newspaper, Susan Root suffered from a form of tinnitus where music and songs played endlessly in her head, day and night. Susan's favourite childhood song has been stuck in her head since 2010.

Classical canines

Does your dog chill out to Chopin or relax to Ravel? A 2014 study revealed that classical music might be the most effective way of calming a dog displaying anxious or fearful behaviour. Led by Dr Lori R. Kogan of Colorado State University, the study found that mutts loved the music of Mozart and his classical chums so much that it appeared to reduce levels of stress in the dogs involved in the trial. Publishing her findings in the *Journal of Veterinary Behavior*, Kogan said that she concluded that classical music was more soothing than any other genre of music or the specially made pet CDs that were designed to calm animals. The study, of which the musical preference of dogs was just a part, included research into the behaviour of 117 dogs of various breeds and took place over four months. Classical music was linked to more relaxed and restful behaviour, while heavy metal was associated with more anxious behaviour.

The dog ate my opera

When Richard Wagner was trying to finish his opera *Die Meistersinger von Nürnberg* his musical genius was tested by the constant whining of a dog. His landlord had tied up a Bulldog named Leo outside the front of the house – and Leo was clearly less than impressed with Wagner's music. Taking pity on the dog, the great composer called a servant to help him free Leo. Much good it did him – the dog promptly bit Wagner on the thumb, triggering an infection. Unable to write for six months, his publisher was not best pleased and must surely have looked upon the excuse 'the dog bit my writing hand' with as much suspicion as the proverbial 'the dog ate my homework'.

Did you know?

George Gershwin's Walking the Dog, *intended to conjure up a jazzy saunter around Manhattan, has a delightful swinging rhythm and a perky clarinet solo. Written for the 1937 film* Shall We Dance, *the piece provided the accompaniment for a scene in which a dog is walked on a luxury liner.*

The pooch hit parade

Patti Page/Lita Roza – 'How Much is That Doggie in the Window?' (1953)

Elvis Presley – 'Hound Dog' (1956)

The Everly Brothers – 'Bird Dog' (1958)

Rufus Thomas – 'Walking the Dog' (1963)

Cat Stevens – 'I Love My Dog' (1966)

Johnny Cash – 'Dirty Old Egg-Sucking Dog' (1966)

The Stooges – 'I Wanna Be Your Dog' (1969)

Lobo – 'Me and You and a Dog Named Boo' (1971)

Led Zeppelin – 'Black Dog' (1971)

Tom T. Hall – 'Old Dogs, Children and Watermelon Wine' (1972)

Donny Osmond – 'Puppy Love' (1972)

Nick Drake – 'Black Eyed Dog' (1974)

Brian and Michael – 'Matchstalk Men and Matchstalk Cats and Dogs' (1978)

George Clinton – 'Atomic Dog' (1983)

Duran Duran – 'Hungry Like the Wolf' (1983)

Kate Bush – 'Hounds of Love' (1985)

Snoop Dogg (featuring Tha Dogg Pound) – 'Doggy Dogg World' (1994)

Pulp – 'Dogs are Everywhere' (1996)

Baha Men – 'Who Let The Dogs Out?' (2000)

Florence + The Machine – 'Dog Days are Over' (2010)

'Daddy Wouldn't Buy Me a Bow Wow'

In 1892 Joseph Tabrar wrote what was to become a traditional song, popular in music halls at the time, that is still sung around camp fires, on long car journeys and in playschools today. It has even been performed by The Muppets!

I love my little cat, I do,
With soft black, silky hair;
It comes with me each day to school,
And sits upon the chair;
When teacher says, 'Why do you bring
That little pet of yours?'
I tell her that I bring my cat
Along with me because –

Daddy wouldn't buy me a bow-wow, bow wow.
Daddy wouldn't buy me a bow-wow, bow wow.
I've got a little cat,
And I'm very fond of that.
But I'd rather have a bow wow, wow, wow, wow, wow.

JOSEPH TABRAR, 'DADDY WOULDN'T BUY ME A BOW WOW'

A howling success

Some dogs really do appear to 'sing'. In July 2014 Oakley the Australian Shepherd dog was filmed 'singing' along to the title song of the Disney blockbuster *Frozen*. Other dogs seem inspired to throw back their heads and howl like *The X Factor* contestants when they hear particular pieces of music. For one poor lady, Michelle O'Brien from Worthing, West Sussex, the song that set her mongrel Bertie off was Elvis Presley's 'Jailhouse Rock'. Easy enough to avoid – or it would have been, but for the fact that Jim, her husband, was an Elvis impersonator. 'The song was one of the best in his repertoire,' explained O'Brien, 'but whenever he rehearsed it Bertie would join in, and eventually I got fed up with the neighbours complaining and he had to drop it from his set. It was the only number that affected Bertie this way – he never even lifted his head from his paws when Jim did 'Hound Dog'!'

Among God's creatures two, the dog and the guitar, have taken all the sizes and all the shapes, in order not to be separated from the man.

ANDRÉS SEGOVIA, CLASSICAL GUITARIST

CHAPTER 10

DOGS IN ENTERTAINMENT

I was haunted by trainers going 'Up, up, up, get up'. You find yourself picking your head up and then realising, they aren't talking to me.

ACTOR JEFF DANIELS, ABOUT WORKING ON THE FILM *101 DALMATIANS*

Many dogs have found fame on the big and small screen, as well as on stage. From movie blockbusters to our favourite soap operas, our love of dogs is another sure-fire way for producers and programme makers to hook us. Featuring in cartoons, adaptations of books and sitcoms, and even starring in their own series or taking the title role in movies, the cute canine factor is not to be underestimated when it comes to matters financial. Making their mark from Hollywood to Broadway and the West End to the BBC, dogs have entertained us since they began appearing in music halls and vaudeville. You could say that introducing dogs into the entertainment industry has been a 'howling' success!

Soap dogs

EastEnders top dogs

Roly (King Poodle) – belonging to the Watts family

Wellard (Belgian Tervuren Shepherd) – belonging to Robbie Jackson

'Little' Willy (Pug) – belonging to Ethel Skinner

Genghis (Irish Wolfhound) – belonging to the Miller family

Lady Di (Bulldog) – belonging to the Carter family

Coronation Street's cutest canines

Eccles (Border Terrier) – most recently owned by the Barlow family

Schmeichel (Great Dane) – owned by Chesney Brown

Monica (Greyhound) – owned by Tyrone Dobbs

Ozzy (Black Labrador) – owned by Maria Connor

Rover (German Shepherd) – owned by Bet Lynch (previously Gilroy)

Other famous soap dogs include Bouncer, a Golden Labrador, and Audrey, the Cairn Terrier, both of whom were much adored in the Australian soap *Neighbours*. Batley, a Yorkshire Terrier, was Edna Birch's baby in *Emmerdale*, while way back in the 1970s Benny in *Crossroads* had a little black and white mutt called Moses.

Did you know?

Emmerdale had the honour of adding a very special trophy to its awards stash. Claiming the first soap animal to win a British Soap Award, Bracken, who played Edna's dog Batley, won Best Exit at the annual awards in 2002. Acting his paws off in the scenes when village vet Paddy diagnosed him with cancer, his ultimate demise left not a dry eye on the couches of the UK.

Pudsey's got talent

Appearing on TV talent show *Britain's Got Talent* in 2012, dancing dog Pudsey, a Border Collie, Bichon Frisé and Chinese Crested Powder Puff cross, and his owner and trainer Ashleigh Butler became the act to beat from the outset. Ashleigh and Pudsey won the hearts of first the nation and then the world – what's not to love about a young girl and a very cute dancing dog whose footwork is as nimble as any *Strictly Come Dancing* contestant's? A book deal, panto roles and *Pudsey the Dog: The Movie* followed, ensuring that this clever little performer could keep himself in top quality bones for the rest of his life.

Blue Peter's *Petra*

It was Britain's favourite kids' TV show of the 1960s and 1970s (and still going strong today), and *Blue Peter* producers wanted to introduce a dog to the show so that young viewers who didn't have a pet could at least have a share in the programme's one. Petra was the first *Blue Peter* dog, introduced in 1962. However, disaster struck when the mongrel died after just one appearance. Not wanting to upset thousands of children, a secret mission to find a lookalike began in earnest. A lookalike was discovered in a London pet shop and Petra remained on the show until 1977, when she retired owing to ill health. News of her death later that year made national headlines. A statue to Petra stands in the *Blue Peter* garden.

Other *Blue Peter* dogs include:

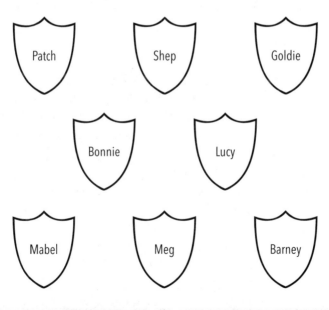

Patch

Shep

Goldie

Bonnie

Lucy

Mabel

Meg

Barney

Animated and adored

As for cartoon dogs, Snoopy, one of the most famous, especially in the USA, started as a comic strip. Brian Griffin, the dog in the outrageous adult cartoon *Family Guy* also has an enormous fan base, while Scooby Doo has been adored by generations. Other famous cartoon dogs include Dougal in *The Magic Roundabout*, Disney's Goofy and Pluto and of course *The Simpson's* dog, Santa's Little Helper. The canine version of Jeeves, Gromit of *Wallace and Gromit,* has won fans the world over as he rescues his hapless master from scrapes and disasters with a mix of calm, cunning and sheer resourcefulness.

Eddie and London

Eddie the Jack Russell Terrier, real name Moose, received fan mail for his role in *Frasier*. The largest of his litter at birth, he went on to become even bigger in terms of his doggy status. *The Littlest Hobo* saw a dog called London, ironically a German Shepherd, having adventure after adventure as he wandered into a different place in each episode. Always helping those having a rough time, when his job is done London always trots off, refusing to be adopted as a pet by those he has helped.

Battersea's waifs and strays

English comedian and presenter Paul O'Grady has gifted London's Battersea Dogs Home the most incredible advertising campaign through his hugely popular television show *For the Love of Dogs*.

Battersea and its satellite sites (in Berkshire and Kent) do incredible work in protecting and caring for dogs (and cats). In 2013 Battersea cared for around 5,421 dogs – and it all began with one determined dog lover. Established in 1860 by Mrs Mary Tealby, who was extremely concerned about the huge number of animals roaming the streets of London, the home was originally called The Temporary Home for Lost & Starving Dogs. It was originally located in Holloway, North London, but the organisation moved to Battersea in 1871 and has been there ever since.

From derelict stables to BAFTA nomination:

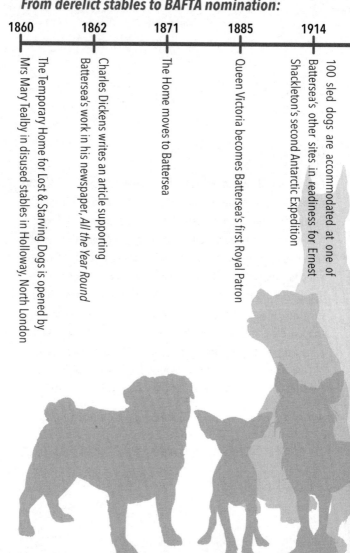

1860	1862	1871	1885	1914
The Temporary Home for Lost & Starving Dogs is opened by Mrs Mary Tealby in disused stables in Holloway, North London	Charles Dickens writes an article supporting Battersea's work in his newspaper, *All the Year Round*	The Home moves to Battersea	Queen Victoria becomes Battersea's first Royal Patron	100 sled dogs are accommodated at one of Battersea's other sites in readiness for Ernest Shackleton's second Antarctic Expedition

Fascinating Battersea facts

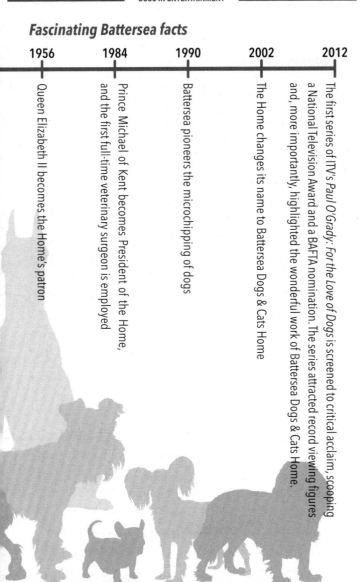

1956

Queen Elizabeth II becomes the Home's patron

1984

Prince Michael of Kent becomes President of the Home, and the first full-time veterinary surgeon is employed

1990

Battersea pioneers the microchipping of dogs

2002

The Home changes its name to Battersea Dogs & Cats Home

2012

The first series of ITV's *Paul O'Grady: For the Love of Dogs* is screened to critical acclaim, scooping a National Television Award and a BAFTA nomination. The series attracted record viewing figures and, more importantly, highlighted the wonderful work of Battersea Dogs & Cats Home.

Leading lady Lassie

> *I have yet to see one completely unspoiled star,*
> *except for the animals – like Lassie.*
> EDITH HEAD, MOVIE DIRECTOR AND DESIGNER

Lassie Come-Home was rewritten as a novel after first being published as a short story by Eric Knight in 1938. The book tells of a courageous Collie that bravely travelled hundreds of miles to return to her young owner. It quickly became a bestseller, and in 1941 Hollywood's MGM studios bought the movie rights for US$10,000. They casted a dog named Pal and the movie premiered in 1943, smashing box office records and delighting both critics and moviegoers. Two of the (human) stars were a young Roddy McDowall and Elizabeth Taylor. More films followed and in 1947 the *Lassie* radio show launched, followed soon after by the television show. Running for 17 years, this award-winning show remains one of the longest running television programmes in history.

Did you know?

Lassie *merchandise from the films or TV shows can be collector's items.* Lassie *collectors can be found all over the world and the market is highly competitive.*

Top dollar Toto

Terry the Cairn Terrier that played Toto in the 1939 film *The Wizard of Oz* was a bitch and not, as the film claims, a male dog. An abandoned dog, Terry was rescued by Carl Spitz, a dog trainer. Landing her first film role in the 1934 romance *Ready for Love*, Terry had a wonderfully successful career and was such a loveable dog that it is said Judy Garland begged to adopt her. Owner Carl Spitz refused, keeping Terry even when she retired from the movies. For her part as Toto in the original film of *The Wizard of Oz* Terry was paid US$125 a week – more than some of the film's human cast members.

Did you know?

Nicknamed 'Rinty', Rin Tin Tin appeared in an impressive 27 Hollywood films and did a great public relations job for German Shepherds. In 1929 Rin Tin Tin received the most votes for the first Academy Award for Best Actor, but it was decided that the award should go to a human – a ruling that surely must have seen his hackles rise.

The play's the thing

On stage some shows call for real dogs to appear. For the stage version of *Chitty Chitty Bang Bang* one scene calls for a pack of dogs to run across the stage on cue. Thanks to good training and plenty of rehearsals this aspect of the production generally goes off without a hitch. However, anyone sitting close to the front with an open bag of sweets runs the risk of being mobbed by the show's canine cast. And when Andrew Lloyd Webber revived *The Wizard of Oz* for the London Palladium in 2011 he cast four Westies – all getting excellent reviews – to alternate playing the role of Toto.

In *Annie* the beloved dog Sandy is a cast member that has, in the past, given the young actress playing the title role a headache. One lady recalls playing the role at the Victoria Palace Theatre in London as a child: 'At one point I was meant to call for Sandy and he would come bounding across the stage to me. Only sometimes he didn't and I'd be left in the middle of the stage practically pleading with the obstinate mutt to leave the wings and come to me. In the end I took to carrying a sausage in my pocket.'

In 2014 the Chichester Festival Theatre in West Sussex announced that it was staging *The Hundred and One Dalmatians*. Spotty dog fans were soon disappointed to learn that the West Sussex venue was not to be overrun by black and white puppies, but instead that members of the resident Youth Theatre would be donning tails and barking.

Did you know?

Hagrid's dog, Fang, played by three different Neapolitan Mastiffs in the Harry Potter *films, was originally brought to life by male dog Monkey in* Harry Potter and the Order of the Phoenix. *Hugo, another of the Mastiffs to have played Fang, memorably made a TV appearance with presenter Fern Britton, during which he drooled on her!*

Top five highest-grossing canine films

 1. *Scooby-Doo* (2002) US$153,294,164 (cinemas only)

 2. *Marley & Me* (2008) US$143,153,751

 3. *101 Dalmatians* (1996) US$136,189,294

 4. *Beverly Hills Chihuahua* (2008) US$94,514,402

 5. *Cats & Dogs* (2001)US$93,385,515

Commercial canines

Many advertisers have used dogs to sell their wares. From insurance companies to toilet roll manufacturers, a cute woofer is a highly effective sales tool. Whether at the movies, online or at home, a clever, sweet-looking or funny dog is a sure-fire way of grabbing our attention – and advertisers know it. Big dogs like St Bernards send a subliminal message that suggests strength, while bouncy dogs like Labradors are used to promote products and services to a family audience.

Paper, paint, Polo and pup food

Generations of loo-roll-thieving Labrador puppies from Andrex have been in more than 130 adverts over the years, since it first aired in 1972. The furry mascot for Dulux paint became so well known that to many people it will always be the Dulux dog rather than an Old English Sheepdog. First appearing in the 1960s, the proverbial shaggy dog story was told in 30 seconds – you too can transform your home with a lick of paint as advertised by this gorgeous fur ball. The first dog to be cast by Dulux was Shepton Dash, which remained the face of the brand for eight years. Shep was succeeded by Fernville Lord Digby. Both dogs were chauffeured to the studio and trained by famous dog trainer Barbara Woodhouse.

Then there was the VW Polo dog. It was seen sitting in the car's passenger seat, being driven by a beautiful woman and belting out 'I'm a Man' by The Spencer Davis Group. The ad was dropped following complaints about suspected animal abuse but these proved to be completely untrue. Viewers who had suggested that the dog was trembling didn't realise that it was in fact standing on a motorised plate to make it look as if it was trembling. In spite of the ad's huge popularity (more than 500,000 hits on YouTube), the ad remained dropped.

In 2012 Britain's first ever TV advert just for dogs was created by Bakers, the dog food manufacturer. The ad included a high-frequency noise above 17,000 Hz, which can be heard only by dogs.

> ### *Did you know?*
>
> *Henry the Bloodhound starred with the late Sir Clement Freud, grandson of Sigmund Freud, in a dog food campaign in the 1960s. Both dog and actor shared the same gloomy expression – the reason a Bloodhound was selected.*

His Master's Voice

An iconic image of the twentieth century, Nipper the dog found fame through a record label. Pictured listening to a gramophone, the smooth-haired Fox Terrier became mascot, logo and trademark for the HMV brand. Painted by Francis Barraud, it wasn't until 1895, three years after Nipper's death, that Francis painted him in the world-famous pose. Entitling the painting *His Master's Voice*, the Royal Academy rejected it, which prompted him to patent the painting instead. He then offered the painting to The Gramophone Company Limited and the rest is musical history.

CHAPTER 11

OUT AND ABOUT: WALKS, TRAVEL AND THE GREAT BLUE YONDER

The average dog is a nicer person than the average person.
ANDY ROONEY, AMERICAN RADIO AND TV WRITER

The companionship of a dog to walk with is surely one of life's greatest pleasures. A prime motivator for getting you out into the fresh air, even when you don't feel like it, a clearing of the cobwebs with a brisk walk almost always improves one's mood and some stick or ball throwing can be a wonderful tension reliever. But 'out and about' extends to travel beyond local public footpaths. Travelling farther afield with your dog, and finding accommodation for it when you need to go away without it, putting your best foot – or paw – forwards sometimes requires a bit of research.

Any woman who does not thoroughly enjoy tramping across the country on a clear frosty morning with a good gun and a pair of dogs does not know how to enjoy life.
ANNIE OAKLEY, SHARPSHOOTER AND STAR OF BUFFALO BILL'S *WILD WEST SHOW*

Walkies!

Walking with your dog is one of life's most pleasurable activities. But in order to enjoy it to the full – and in order to be a good, law-abiding dog owner – you need to be aware of the laws of the land when it comes to dogs and the environment. The UK's Clean Neighbourhoods and Environment Act 2005 gives local authorities the power to impose Dog Control Orders. The failure to scoop your dog's poop, not keeping it on a lead in areas that have signage asking you to do so, staying out of areas that are signposted as 'No Dogs' – all essentially failures to comply with common sense – could see you facing a fixed penalty notice. Take care to keep your dog on a short lead near livestock and ideally plan walks that put plenty of space between you and fields of sheep, horses or cattle.

Did you know?

When on a short lead your dog should walk near your foot. The standard heel *position is to your left, with your dog's head in line with your left leg, waiting for your signals.*

Did you know?

It takes very little time for a dog left in a car on a hot day to become extremely unwell. Never leave a dog in the car in the summer for more than a couple of minutes and report anyone who does.

Leading astray

A retractable lead for open spaces allows your dog a certain amount of freedom while still leaving you in full control. Training classes will make a huge difference to your dog's behaviour on the lead. Never let your dog off the lead unless it is safe and legal for you to do so and you are completely confident in its return.

Picnics are an extremely tempting prospect for dogs. They need to learn that eating anything on a walk, offered or found, is forbidden. Apart from a being a bad habit to develop, tragically there have been cases of poisoned food being deliberately discarded for dogs to find and eat.

Tess's travels

Walking the coastline of Britain in its entirety with her dog Tess, in her book *Two Feet, Four Paws*, Spud Talbot-Ponsonby recounts her thoughts on the final leg of the journey:

Tess had waited on the muddy paths of Cornwall when I had thought I could go no further. She had experienced my Highland euphoria, and leapt the peat gullies with sheer joie de vivre; she had pounded main roads, being sprayed by polluted puddles; she had walked hundreds of miles of empty beach; she had fallen in rock pools, and communicated with foxes; she had learnt the laws of nature, and had learnt to love the sea; she had played in the snow, and sweated many miles; she had walked through numerous eight-hour-long deluges; she had chewed mayors' ears, and eaten their teas; she had made photographers despair and wrestled with policemen; she had made homeless people smile; she had loved the drivers and made them each feel special; she had slept in castles, Butlin's, grand hotels, haunted spare rooms, mobile homes, guest houses and top floor flats. She was a star.

Did you know?

Barking Sands Beach on the Hawaiian island of Kauai is so named because its unusually dry sand is said to sound like a barking dog when walked on.

Long walk checklist

- ☑ Retractable lead
- ☑ Dog treats
- ☑ First aid kit including saline eye wash, foil blanket, tweezers and alcohol-free wipes and a bandage
- ☑ A collapsible water bowl and a small bottle of water in case you get lost and there is no fresh water source
- ☑ Mobile telephone (fully charged and with charger so you can recharge en route)
- ☑ Map
- ☑ Binoculars

Indoor walkies

Following the American trend, a Cardiff business woman opened the first indoor dog walking centre in 2014. Action Petz allows dogs and their owners to enjoy a walk whatever the weather, when for under £5 they can enjoy the space of a converted warehouse to walk on fake grass, play with toys and in tunnels and even have forty winks in the designated snooze areas.

Running with the pack

If you're a runner, or even just a jogger, then a canine companion can be the perfect partner for your sport. Obviously you need to own a breed that enjoys a good run – a Pekinese might mean that it takes you as long to go around the block as it takes the chap in the metal diving suit to finish the London Marathon – but so long as you are sensible and observe some basic guidelines then a 'dog jog' can be a great way of combining exercise for you and your dog.

To run with a dog you should:

First ensure that both you and your dog are fit enough to run. Ease into running gently, with a short distance that can be built up over time. You wouldn't ask an overweight or unfit friend to do 11 kilometres (7 miles) straight off, so don't ask the same of your dog.

Start off with your dog on a lead so that it understands what is expected and gets used to the concept of running beside you. Dogs are clever and some runners report that when their dogs see them pulling on running shoes rather than wellingtons their enthusiasm to get out and get going goes into overdrive!

Don't run in the dark. Even if you are both wearing high visibility clothing, it is safer to keep to daylight hours when running with a mutt.

Take care when running with younger dogs. Running is a repetitive activity and this can cause damage to your dog's joints, resulting in problems in later life. If in any doubt, speak to your vet first.

Keep it clean! You might have to break your stride, but cleaning up after your pup is still your responsibility even when you're trying to beat a personal best. Make sure you tuck poo bags into a (zip-up) pocket before you begin your run.

Carry enough water for you and your dog, or make sure you plot a route that takes you via a shop or pub so that you can rehydrate. If it's really hot then maybe go solo – dogs will struggle to run comfortably in heat.

A running buddy who will never let you down by bailing on you, will have better stamina than any human running partner and who will never grumble if you want to get up early and run at first light, your woofer could help you to become as fit as the proverbial butcher's dog. You might have to throw the occasional ball en route, but hey, look at it as an additional element to your workout.

Staying over with Rover

There are many dog-friendly hotels to be found around the world and a quick internet search will identify suitable places for you and Rover to rest your heads and have your bowls filled. Take time to find out exactly what each establishment offers – do you need to take dog bedding, and are dogs restricted just to the bedroom or are they permitted in the bar area, for instance. Self-catering accommodation offers even more flexibility, with some places even dedicated to dog owners and their furry friends. Bed and Basket in the English Cornish countryside, for example, provides top-notch self-catering accommodation and comes complete with doggy welcome pack, log burning stoves and even a doggy throw for the sofa if your pooch is 'allowed up'.

Kennels

Finding a home-from-home for your dog when you go on holiday can be stressful. Personal recommendations are always valuable when looking for a good quality berth for your dog, so ask friends and your vet if they have any particular advice, but always go and visit potential kennels first. Ideally you should visit at least three kennels before you make your final choice, and go armed with a list of questions and considerations. Many kennels welcome people without a prior appointment, so you see the place in its regular day-to-day state. This is always a good sign.

Kennels must be licensed by the local authority and should display a valid certificate. They may also be a member of a professional body such as the Pet Care Trust (PCT) and hold references for local vets. Don't be afraid to enquire about their credentials.

Take a good look at the places your dog will be playing, sleeping and exercising. Ask how often and for how long dogs are walked each day. If a dog is not given adequate walks when it is already unsettled being away from home it can become extremely stressed and anxious.

Kennels should be clean and aired – you shouldn't be able to smell anything unpleasant. Pens should be safe and secure and animals in residence at the time of your visit should be well looked after and relaxed.

Reducing the risk of infections being spread should be paramount at a boarding kennels and any proprietor of such an establishment should be able to confirm that facilities keep dogs from different households apart so that they do not become vulnerable to diseases such as kennel cough.

Ask questions about anything you're not sure of and take careful note of whether the staff are welcoming, kind and experienced. Other questions worth asking include:

- Is a vet always on call?
- Can they meet special requirements such as grooming?
- If you have more than one dog, can they stay together?

Good kennels tend to get booked up well in advance, so book early.

Your contact details should be taken in full when you entrust your dog to a boarding facility. You should also be able to leave written details of your preferred vet's contact details, an emergency contact for someone in the event that you can't be reached and details of any specific dietary and exercise needs.

Alternatively, if you really would prefer for your dog to have a 'proper' home, it is worth considering a foster family. Organisations such as Borrow My Doggy offer holiday cover, matching your dog to a 'foster' family who for whatever reason cannot have a full-time dog, but who love the occasional canine companion.

International travel

To travel abroad with your dog you must meet the entry requirements for the country you're going to or coming from. When you enter or return to the UK from another EU or non-EU listed country your pet needs to meet the entry requirements. Dogs must be microchipped, have had a rabies vaccination (a wait of 21 whole days from the date of the vaccination before travelling is required) and tapeworm treatment and have their own pet passport or third country official veterinary certificate. You are obliged to use an approved transport company and an approved route unless you're travelling between the UK and the Republic of Ireland. Entering the UK from an unlisted country has further requirements, including blood tests. Quarantine laws may apply, depending on where you are travelling from. Make sure you are fully apprised of the requirements well ahead of any planned journey.

Dog air miles

When English socialite Lady Victoria Hervey was booked to appear on Channel 4's winter sports competition The Jump *in 2015 she insisted that producers fly her dog, a Norfolk Terrier called D'Artagnan, out to be with her whenever – and wherever – filming took place. From her base in Los Angeles, D'Artagnan covered some 28,000 km (17,500 miles) as her mistress trained for and appeared in the show, in which contestants learn to perform ski jumps.*

CHAPTER 12

BRAVE, INTELLIGENT AND LOYAL: ALL DOGS BRIGHT AND BEAUTIFUL

The guard dog was incorruptible; the police dog dependable; the messenger dog reliable. The human watchman might be bought; not so the dog. The soldier sentinel might fall asleep; never the dog. The battlefield runner might fail… but not the dog, to his last breath would follow the line of duty.

ERNEST HAROLD BAYNES, *ANIMAL HEROES OF THE GREAT WAR*

Canine cadets of history

Bravery on the battlefield, in minefields and on patrol for the armed forces and police – there's no shortage of stories about the courage and intelligence of our four-legged friends. Dogs in the army go back to the time of Christopher Columbus's return to the Americas in 1495. Bringing dogs with him, he called them 'the most fearsome weapon of all'. Attacked by the Taino, the indigenous people of Hispaniola, an island in the West Indies, Columbus unleashed his 'fearsome weapons' to first terrify and then disembowel. During the American Revolutionary War, dogs were used as sentry dogs. Guarding groceries, guns and captives, the woofers also raised the alarm when required to do so.

During the Seven Years War, Russian dogs were utilised as messengers and, horrifically, as suicide bombers. Napoleon used dogs as sentries at the gates of Alexandria, while the first recorded American Canine Corps dates back to the Seminole War of 1835. In 1842 in Florida and Louisiana the army used Bloodhounds to track American Indians and runaway slaves. But it was the Germans who established the first military school for training war dogs, opening the kennel door to cadets of the German Army in 1884.

In World War One, dogs played many roles, including finding bodies on the battlefield and identifying the wounded. The bigger dogs would drag the bodies of men to safety. They were also used to deliver messages to the front line, being faster and harder to aim at than a man. In 1918 thousands of dogs from The Battersea Home made up the first batch of recruits of the War Dog School. Trained to become messengers, sentries and munitions carriers, these extraordinary recruits played a key role in the war. Dogs were also trained for war in World War Two.

That's the way to do it, Judy

During World War Two an English Pointer, a bitch called Judy, served on a Royal Navy vessel where she was able to detect the sound of hostile aircraft far sooner than her fellow human crew members. Alas the vessel was a casualty of battle and sank. The crew were captured and carted off to a prisoner of war camp. Resourceful Judy somehow wormed her way into the camp and helped her buddies by bringing them scavenged scraps. Japanese guards tried several times to kill her, but Judy was too wily. After the war RAF serviceman Frank Williams pestered the authorities to register Judy as an official prisoner of war and she remains the only animal in history to be accorded the status.

This soldier, I realised, must have had friends at home and in his regiment; yet he lay there deserted by all except his dog. I looked on, unmoved, at battles which decided the future of nations. Tearless, I had given orders which brought death to thousands. Yet here I was stirred, profoundly stirred, stirred to tears. And by what? By the grief of one dog.

NAPOLEON BONAPARTE, ON THE DISCOVERY OF A DOG
KEEPING WATCH OVER ITS DEAD MASTER

Dogs of war by numbers

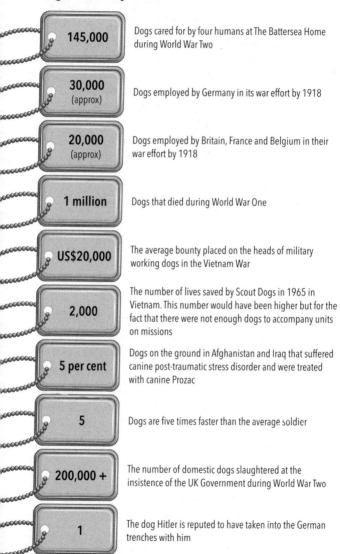

145,000 — Dogs cared for by four humans at The Battersea Home during World War Two

30,000 (approx) — Dogs employed by Germany in its war effort by 1918

20,000 (approx) — Dogs employed by Britain, France and Belgium in their war effort by 1918

1 million — Dogs that died during World War One

US$20,000 — The average bounty placed on the heads of military working dogs in the Vietnam War

2,000 — The number of lives saved by Scout Dogs in 1965 in Vietnam. This number would have been higher but for the fact that there were not enough dogs to accompany units on missions

5 per cent — Dogs on the ground in Afghanistan and Iraq that suffered canine post-traumatic stress disorder and were treated with canine Prozac

5 — Dogs are five times faster than the average soldier

200,000 + — The number of domestic dogs slaughtered at the insistence of the UK Government during World War Two

1 — The dog Hitler is reputed to have taken into the German trenches with him

> ### Did you know?
>
> *Military dogs are put through rigorous testing before they are deemed suitable for service. This includes putting dogs into simulated war situations and subjecting them to gunfire and explosions. Dogs must be able to navigate underground tunnels, be fit and agile enough to climb ladders and walls and generally be as brave and fearless as the most intrepid human soldier.*

What counts is not necessarily the size of the dog in the fight – it's the size of the fight in the dog.

DWIGHT D. EISENHOWER, US PRESIDENT 1953–1961

Liam and Theo

When explosive search dog handler Lance Corporal Liam Tasker was paired with Theo, a Springer Spaniel cross, the two soon became inseparable. During a five-month stint in Afghanistan the pair saved countless lives, finding more bombs than any other soldier/dog pairing. But in February 2011, 26-year-old Liam was shot dead by the Taliban. Theo, who was not quite two years old and in great health, suffered a seizure and died just days later. Dying of a broken heart seems to be the only explanation as to why this dog, as brave and true as his master, simply gave up on life.

He is the one person to whom I can talk without the conversation coming back to war.

DWIGHT D. EISENHOWER ON HIS SCOTTIE DOG

Taking a bullet

When a man suddenly appeared brandishing an AK-47 at him in Afghanistan in 2010, US Staff Sergeant John Mariana simply let his dog Bronco, an eight-year-old Belgian Malinois, off his lead. The dog attacked the enemy, who retaliated by firing. Bronco ran off but when Mariana found him he realised that Bronco had literally taken a bullet for him. Passing through the side of his mouth, the bullet had seriously damaged his muzzle and nose bone. The gutsy hound also had fractured teeth. After several gruelling surgeries, during which Mariana stayed by his dog's side, further surgery was needed back in America. For five long months man and dog were separated. When the pair were finally reunited both human and canine soldiers cried with joy. 'He worked for me because he loved me and I love him. And I really believe that he knew that,' Mariana is quoted as saying.

To err is human, to forgive, canine.

Anonymous

Did you know?

During the days of the Roman Empire teams of dogs were kitted out with armour or vicious spiked collars before being sent onto the battlefield to attack the enemy.

> ### Did you know?
>
> - In his campaigns Attila the Hun used giant Molossian dogs, predecessors of the Mastiff.
> - In the Middle Ages dogs were often used to defend caravans.

Stubby the hero

The US army did not favour the use of dogs during World War One. A couple of hundred belonged to the Allies, but America did not employ anything like as many as countries in Europe did. However, one all-American Terrier brought great glory to the US army. A stray, Stubby, as he affectionately became known, was wandering through an army training session at Yale Field in Connecticut. The dog became friendly with all the soldiers, but one especially, Corporal Robert Conroy, fell hook, line and sinker for the little dog. Christening him Stubby, most likely because of the size and shape of the dog's tail, it is said that the good Corporal Conroy was so fond of Stubby that when he was posted to the Western Front he smuggled Stubby into France with him. He was discovered too late, and Stubby was permitted to stay with his master and became a part of the 102nd Infantry, 26th Division, known as the Yankee Division. Plunged into the horrors of war the brave dog was present at battles including Château-Thierry, the Marne and St Mihiel. He survived injuries from shrapnel and gas attacks and is reported to have been so well-known for his guts and loyalty that he was treated like a proper soldier in Red Cross hospitals.

Detecting gas and alerting and comforting his comrades, he even brought down a German spy who attempted to tiptoe into the camp at night, by biting his leg and giving the troops time to imprison the unfortunate chap. Declared a hero, Stubby received more medals than any other soldier dog and was awarded lifetime membership of the American Legion.

His angry howl while a battle raged and his mad canter from one part of the lines to another indicated realization. But he seemed to know that the greatest service he could render was comfort and cheerfulness.

EXTRACTED FROM STUBBY'S OBITUARY IN *THE NEW YORK TIMES* FOLLOWING HIS DEATH IN 1926

Did you know?

In World War One, Mercy dogs were trained to find casualties on the battlefields. Carrying medical supplies, soldiers who could tend to their own wounds helped themselves to the bandages and other first aid equipment. Those so badly wounded that they were certain to die surely took some comfort in the presence of a Mercy dog as they prepared for the end.

Love conquers all

In addition to seeing active service the companionship, affection and faithfulness that dogs have offered soldiers throughout history remains invaluable. Psychologically, the comforting presence of a dog was a welcome – essential, some would say – distraction from the grim brutality of war. In recent conflict, Layla was found by a group of US Marines while on foot patrol in Afghanistan. While the puppy had no military training to offer, she gave the soldiers one thing they desperately needed: love. Always ready to greet them with affection and a wagging tail when they returned to camp, she was an instant ray of sunshine that made their dangerous and highly pressurised circumstances more bearable.

The dog is a gentleman; I hope to go to his heaven, not man's.
MARK TWAIN, AUTHOR AND HUMORIST

'For Gallantry' – the Dickin Medal

A bronze medallion inscribed with the words 'For Gallantry' and 'We Also Serve', the Dickin Medal hangs on a green, dark brown and pale blue striped ribbon. The stripes represent water, earth and air – the naval, land and air forces. Established during World War Two by the founder of the PDSA (People's Dispensary for Sick Animals) Maria Dickin CBE, the Dickin Medal was introduced to honour animals' devotion to man and duty, and is awarded to animals displaying bravery in the line of duty while serving or associated with any branch of the armed forces or civil defence units.

Two dogs that earned the Dickin Medal in 2002 were Salty and Roselle, Labrador guide dogs. When the terrorist attack of 9/11 was made on the World Trade Center, these remarkable dogs remained steadfastly by their blind owners' sides, bravely leading them down over 70 floors and to safety. Through smoke, mass panic and falling debris, the dogs did not falter. Salty and Roselle were also honoured by the UK's The Guide Dogs for the Blind Association.

Not just brave in battle

Using their wonderful noses to sniff out bombs, casualties, drugs and baddies, it's not just in battle that dogs save lives. Pet dogs have often been honoured for acts of heroism, instinctively leaping to the defence of their human friends or alerting their families to imminent danger such as fire or, in 11-year-old Austin Forman's case, prowling cougars.

When Austin went outside to collect wood for his family's wood-burning furnace at their home in British Columbia, Canada, Angel the 18-month-old Golden Retriever went with him. But the dog was acting out of character; cautious and obviously alert to something that Austin couldn't see. That's when a cougar tried to pounce on the boy. Leaping directly into the beast's path, Angel managed to fend it off until a local police constable shot it. Angel needed major surgery for head injuries but recovered well. Understandably Austin was quick to empty his piggy bank and buy his Angel the biggest steak the butcher could supply.

Did you know?

The first cloned dogs, six Canadian Labradors, all became sniffer dogs for South Korea's customs service.

Swimming saviours

On holiday with his family, black Labrador–Golden Retriever cross Yaron, a guide dog, turned his paw to lifeguard duties. On the beach one day, one of the family's little girls, Charlotte, toppled off her bodyboard into the sea. Swept away by the current and with no lifejacket, she began to panic. Yaron jumped into the sea and began swimming towards her. Swimming in circles around her, enabling her to catch hold of his collar, Yaron calmly towed Charlotte safely back to shore. Yaron's heroics saw him named as the Beyond the Call of Duty Guide Dog of the Year 2008 at the American Guide Dog of the Year Awards.

And while English Bulldogs are not famed for their swimming skills, it appears that they do have tender hearts. Heaving himself into a lake, Napoleon bravely swam out to retrieve a sack containing six abandoned kittens. Although too late to save two of the kitties, four survived thanks to this courageous and sweet-natured dog.

Another canine sea saviour is Patty. When Ray Fogg was duck hunting in the freezing waters of the North Atlantic in 2001 he was accompanied by Patty, a yellow Labrador Retriever. When the boat suddenly capsized, man and dog were both in serious danger; the icy temperature of the water alone could have seen them perish and then there was the strong current to battle against. But Patty took matters into her own paws. Allowing Ray to grab hold of her tail, courageous Patty doggy-paddled furiously against the current, forcing herself and her human cargo through it and, eventually, to dry land. Rescued by game wardens later on that evening, Patty truly proved that Labrador Retrievers are indeed natural water dogs.

Snakes and dog heroes

Zoey, a two-kilogram (five-pound) Chihuahua from Colorado, proved in 2007 that you're never too small to make a big difference – the difference between life and death, in fact. With a rattlesnake making a beeline for a one-year-old baby, gutsy little Zoey decided it was time to show the reptile that if you mess with a handbag dog you *become* the handbag. Zoey was bitten by the snake just above her eye, but the brave wee woofer recovered and was hailed a hero. The snake was killed by Zoey's owner.

Similarly, Leo, a Standard Poodle from Texas, saved his young master's life by throwing himself between a 167-centimetre (5.5-feet) diamondback rattlesnake and the boy, allowing the child to escape. Badly bitten by the venomous reptile, the aptly named Leo, the lionhearted hound, did eventually make a complete recovery.

Doctor Dog

In the spotlight during the American Society for the Prevention of Cruelty to Animals' Dog of the Year awards in 2007, Toby the Golden Retriever from Maryland was recognised for his amazing lifesaving skills. When Toby's owner Debbie Parkhurst started to choke on a piece of apple she began to panic – the apple was lodged in her windpipe. When he saw that Debbie was struggling for breath quick-thinking Toby performed the canine version of the Heimlich manoeuvre – he leapt hard onto her chest. Forcing the wedged apple loose, Debbie owes her life to this amazing Doctor Dog.

Did you know?

Barry, a St Bernard from Switzerland, is believed to be the breed's most successful rescuer, having saved more than 40 lives.

Bite-sized brilliance

Belle the beagle from Florida is proof, were proof needed, that dogs really are intelligent as well as loyal. When her diabetic owner Kevin Weaver had a seizure and collapsed in 2005, Belle's training as a diabetic assistance dog kicked straight in. Grabbing Kevin's mobile phone the little dog bit down on the number 9, the stored number for the emergency services. With his blood sugar having dropped to a potentially fatal level, Belle undoubtedly saved her owner's life – an act she was rightly honoured for when she became the first dog ever to win the VITA Wireless Samaritan Award, an award given to someone who uses a mobile telephone to save a life, prevent a crime or help in an emergency.

One day I would like to be the person my dog thinks I am.
ANONYMOUS

And finally… Dad's shadow

When Janis's mother was ill in hospital, Janis and her husband Bill moved in with her dad to keep him company. This is her story of Zoe, the family's loyal and faithful mutt.

Sadly, Mum passed away on Hogmanay and her funeral was ten days later. A couple of days after that, Bill and I packed our things to go home. When we were ready, we called Zoe to get into the car. She was standing beside Dad and took a step back, as if to say, 'I'm staying here.' From then she stayed with Dad, lying on the landing when he was in the bathroom and sleeping in his bedroom. One night she nudged him awake and he couldn't understand why until he went to the loo and heard the peep from the smoke alarm, letting him know the battery was flat. We moved up to near Aberdeen and the following year Dad moved in with us. Zoe obviously still thought it was her job to look after him and was still his shadow.

Zoe went to the great woodland in the sky in 2014 but, as so many loyal and faithful canine friends do, she remains in the grateful hearts of her human family.

RESOURCES

Animal Search UK – www.animalsearchuk.co.uk

Association of Pet Behaviour Counsellors – www.apbc.org.uk

Battersea Dogs & Cats Home – www.battersea.org.uk

Bulldog Rescue & Rehoming – www.bulldogrescue.org.uk

Canine Partners – www.caninepartners.co.uk

Dogs Trust – www.dogstrust.org.uk

German Shepherd Dog Rescue – www.germanshepherdrescue.co.uk

The Guide Dogs for the Blind Association – www.guidedogs.org.uk

Guild of Dog Trainers – www.godt.org.uk

Hearing Dogs for Deaf People – www.hearingdogs.org.uk

The Kennel Club – www.thekennelclub.org.uk

Labrador Retriever Rescue – www.labrador-rescue.org.uk

Lost and Stolen Dogs – www.doglost.co.uk (national register for missing dogs)

Medical alert dogs (Europe) – www.servicedogseurope-uk.com

Medical Detection Dogs – www.medicaldetectiondogs.org.uk

Medivet Animal Trust (supporting those in need of financial assistance with vet bills) – www.ma-trust.org

People's Dispensary for Sick Animals (PDSA) – www.pdsa.org.uk

Retired Greyhound Trust – www.retiredgreyhounds.co.uk

Royal Society for the Prevention of Cruelty to Animals (RSPCA) – www.rspca.org.uk

Siberian Husky Club of Great Britain – www.siberianhuskyclub.org.uk

Out and about

Animal training for film and TV – www.rockwoodanimals.com

Bed and Basket: Self-catering accommodation, Cornwall, England –
www.bedandbasket.co.uk

Borrow my Doggy – www.borrowmydoggy.com

Crufts – www.crufts.org.uk

Dog-friendly pubs – www.doggiepubs.org.uk

Holidays in the UK with your dog – www.dogpeople.co.uk

Further reading

Coile, Caroline *The Dog Breed Bible* (2007, Barron's)

Common, Jane *Phileas Dogg's Guide to Dog-Friendly Holidays in
Britain* (2014, Constable)

Dilger, Andrew *Dash: Bitch of the Year* (2011, Summersdale)

Edward, Olivia *The More I See of Men, the More I Love My Dog*
(2002, Summersdale)

Fogle, Bruce *RSPCA New Complete Dog Training Manual* (2006,
Dorling Kindersley)

Fogle, Bruce *The New Encyclopedia of the Dog* (2000, Prentice Hall)

Hawkins, Barrie *Twenty Wagging Tales: Our Year of Rehoming
Orphaned Dogs* (2009, Summersdale)

Holt, Ben *Dog Heroes: True Stories of Canine Courage* (2009,
Summersdale)

Jenkins, Garry *A Home of Their Own: The Heart-warming 150-year
History of Battersea Dogs & Cats Home* (2010, Bantam Press)

Webster, Richard *Is Your Pet Psychic? Developing Psychic
Communication with Your Pet* (2002, Llewellyn Publications)